32 Weeks of Inspiring Devotions
to Fuel Your First Year of College

CHAPLAIN
PUBLISHING

RISE

Library of Congress Control Number: 2014906550
ISBN: 978-1-941549-01-8

Chaplain Publishing
3104 County Road 7520
Lubbock, TX 79423
www.chaplainpublishing.com

Cover photo by Brittany Boner
Cover and text design: NiTROhype Creative
www.nitrohype.com

Printed in the United States of America

With thanks

to

my dear friends from the Baptist Student Union at Southeast Missouri State University. Thank you for encouraging me to Rise and follow Jesus

and

to my family who sent me to college with a little bit of money and a lot of prayers

and

to my husband—marrying you was the best decision I made in college.

Table of Contents

Table of Contents

Preface

Each year our church holds a special service to recognize our high school graduates. Even when I was new to the church and didn't know any of the graduates, I would find myself weeping through the recognitions. There is something so touching about seeing a church family publicly wrap their arms around their graduates one last time before they are sent off to face the future.

This book is born out of a desire to allow writers from all over the country to metaphorically wrap their arms around high school graduates they will probably never meet. If you don't have a church family to send you off, consider the person who gave this book to you or told you about it to be sending you off with love.

My goal was to find 80 authors who would submit devotions. As He generally does, God provided even more than I asked. He prompted 92 people to put fingers to keyboard and pour out their heart for college students just like you. When you meet someone, the first thing they tell you is their first name. I have decided to list the author bios and the author index by first name. Consider these writers your new friends. They are not all professional writers. Some of them are housewives. Some are college students. Some are pastors. Some are grandmothers. But they are all followers of Jesus. And they are all rooting for you!

Introduction

I vividly remember the day my parents dropped me off at college. We had moved my meager belongings into the dorm earlier in the day and it was time for them to head home. My boyfriend at the time had driven down with them, so I had to say goodbye to them and him. They pulled up in front of the administration building where I needed to turn in some papers. I hugged the three of them and got out of the car. I walked into the building, excited about my new adventure.

The three of them watched me walk up the paved pathway into the building and my future without them.

I didn't look back.

My parents later told me this made an impression on them. At first they were a little hurt that I didn't demonstrate my continued need for them by looking back to the car as I walked to the building. As they thought about it, though, they were also proud of the self-assured and confident young woman who was ready to face her future.

What they didn't know, though, was that there would be many times I would look back. Each semester I would have at least one day when I would call home in tears telling my mom that I wasn't cut out for college, I couldn't handle the pressure of the classes and assignments, and all I wanted was to come home and curl up in my nice warm bed. She would reassure me that I was indeed cut out for college and I would make it.

On days when I really missed home and just wanted to see a familiar face, my dad would concoct some reason to drive the hour and a half to take me out for lunch. On the rare weekends when I came home, my church song leader chose all my favorites to sing.

I still needed my parents and my hometown. Moving away to college didn't change my need for a relationship with them, but it did change the dynamics of that relationship.

Exactly 20 years has passed from the day they dropped me off at college. I am not the same girl they moved into the dorm. The four years I spent at college changed me, and it will change you. The challenge is deciding which changes to embrace and which ones to reject. Many devotional authors have chosen to write about these changes and how to navigate them with wisdom.

Every contributor to this devotional has prayed for you. I asked them to begin praying for you even before they started writing the devotionals they would submit. Every week this year I am going to ask them to pray for something specifically for you. This is a pivotal time in your life, and my overall prayer is that you would use the next 4 years to either begin or deepen your walk with Jesus. He will walk with you through the aching loneliness. He will help you survive the mounting pressure of papers, projects, and tests all due at once. He will empower you to stand up to wrong philosophies and negative peer pressure. He will direct your steps as you choose your classes, friends, and career. He wants to be your closest companion at college and forever, but you have to choose Him.

We wrote this devotion with one prayer in mind. Our prayer is that you would choose Jesus today and tomorrow and every day after that.

So as you wake up each morning, read your devotional for the day and—Rise.

As the pressures of college life weigh you down—Rise.

When you are missing home and afraid to find new friends—Rise.

As you prepare for your future—Rise.

When you don't think you can continue to follow Jesus one more step—Rise.

I rise before dawn and cry for help;
I have put my hope in your word. Psalm 119:147 NIV

A Table for Two

Be strong and courageous. Do not be afraid or terrified because of them, for the LORD your God goes with you; he will never leave you nor forsake you.
Deuteronomy 31:6 NIV

Who will I eat with? A ridiculous concern, but at the top of my list. I imagined feeling alone on a campus of thousands. I wanted to be invisible—no, I wanted friends. I wanted to do well, but wanted to enjoy my freedom.

Emotions swished around my stomach. I didn't know what I wanted; I just knew I was supposed to be confident. I was the first in my family to go to college. My parents and siblings were so proud; I felt like I was going to throw-up.

My anxiety centered around social issues. I liked periods of quietness. If my roommate was a constant talker, it could be tough to get along. I was a mess inside, but I looked great in my new jeans.

I knew I could call home if I needed money, but I was determined to make the budget work. My parents were spending a lot to send me here. Hundreds of miles away from home, I would learn to cope in my new environment.

Well, I acclimated to my surroundings in less time than I worried about them. My roommate turned out fine. We survived freshman year together, learned the ropes, then went our separate ways.

I had to step out of my comfort zone to meet new people. It surprised me how much I missed home, friends, and familiar things. One night as I sat alone at dinner—which was no big deal after all—I sensed the presence of God. Words can't explain, but I had an awareness that He was there. A warm embrace enveloped me from the inside out.

I continued to sense His presence. When I was alone, which turned out to be rare, I knew He was with me. I imagined Him across the table when I ate. My confidence grew knowing, He would never leave me nor forsake me. I was grateful for that foundation. I was still shakable, but He was not. So I leaned on His steady companionship. It gave me pause when I knew I should think twice. And forgave my youth, when I knew I crossed the line.

Depend on God. He will be your Rock!

Above all Else

Young People can live a clean life by obeying your word...I treasure your word above all else: it keeps me from sinning against you. I will study your teachings and follow your footsteps. Psalm 119:9, 11, 15 CEV

There are a lot of decisions right now. What courses and electives to take? How do I spend my money to provide for my needs? Which classmates are positive influences? Should I attend this party? A classmate asked me to do something, but should I?

This year may be one to stand at the crossroads of decision-making in obedience to Jesus. From personal experience, if I am not studying God's word and allowing Him to mold my decisions, I'm in a very precarious spot. King David understood this. He had to live with some very serious and sad decisions he had made. Because of that, he encourages others to treasure "God's word above all else: it keeps me from sinning against you."

I understand the pressures of college-life decisions. Peer Pressure weighs heavy. We want to have friends, be liked by classmates, obtain good grades, and have fun. Maybe for the first time in your life, you are not under your parent's roof and rules. This new freedom is exciting and "besides, no one will know what I am doing. It isn't that bad." I learned that if it didn't line up with God's heart, it can be.

I cannot undo my unwise choices with past relationships and trying to live up to others standards. What I can do is encourage you to live life freely in God.

True happiness at college can be as David said, "Obeying your instructions brings as much happiness as being rich." Living a life of integrity helped me realize obeying God's Word gave true peace and happiness. Other things will fall into place when that happens like true friends, wise decisions about studies, and extra-curricular activities.

Above all else, with studying your career choice, first study God's word so you follow His footsteps. King David writes in verse 6 from the same chapter, "Thinking about your commands will keep me from doing some foolish thing." The result is knowing the Truth.

What decisions are you facing this week? Claim Psalm 119 and watch the adventure unfold.

Sculpted from Nothing

You know exactly how I was made, bit by bit, how I was sculpted from nothing into something. Psalm 139:15 Message

Many believe that science can explain the world and that the more we understand science, the more we will see there is no place for God. As a physical therapy student, however, I was captivated by how God designed the human body.

All first year students in the medical field – therapists, dentists, doctors – did a full year in the anatomy labs working with cadavers. It was pretty amazing at just 17 years old, to be touching and seeing the inner workings of the human body.

There were strict rules about behavior in the labs, such as treating these bodies with respect. But this 'respect' has never come close to my sense of awe in discovering God's creation. I found the more I learned, the more I marveled at how God could even think up something as complex as a living, working body. All the sciences come together to make the simplest action occur – chemistry to burn energy; physics and biomechanics so the angle of leverage moves the limb; physiology to monitor the effects and adapt if needed.

Each little bit works together with the rest perfectly. The muscles of the body fit together economically. Not only does a little groove in the bone carry a nerve round a corner, but the bony ridge adds protection. The organs in the abdominal cavity are shaped to fit round each other. There are just six muscles round each eyeball, yet they work together to pull our eye in any direction we choose – amazingly, we learn to move our eyes without giving it any thought.

There is much we do not understand about the body – I hope we never do. Science can never replace God.

Never think you are just a body, a biological machine, an animal, or a collection of cells. The Bible tells us "we are fearfully and wonderfully made."

I have a deep sense of awe when I work with the human body: not just the physical body but the personality, the intellect, the spirit that dwells in it. By respecting others, in my friendships, in my work of treating people, and in how I speak about them, I am honoring God by honoring his creation.

You Are Never Alone

I can remember as if it happened yesterday. My first day at college. I came from a high school that had a total enrollment of 2,000 students to a college that had over 2,000 in the freshmen class. Overwhelmed doesn't begin to describe how I felt. I didn't know one single person. I was lonely and all alone. It is one of the worst feelings—to be alone and lonely. Especially in the midst of a crowd – orientation, my first class, a meeting of the sorority from which I hoped to receive an invitation. Wherever I went, I felt completely alone, as if I was invisible. No one saw me. And if by chance they did see me, they didn't acknowledge me, much less the loneliness I felt.

Perhaps you find yourself in a similar situation. You've just arrived on campus of the college you dreamed of attending. But it's not off to such a great start. You don't know anyone. You can't find the classroom buildings. You haven't seen your roommate since she checked in two days ago.

The reality is you are not alone. God is beside you every step you take, every breath you breathe. There are several verses in the Bible that assure us we are never alone, but a verse that states it so well is Hebrews 13:5 from the Amplified Bible: "for He [God] Himself has said, I will not in any way fail you nor give you up nor leave you without support. [I will] not, [I will] not, [I will] not in any degree leave you help-less nor forsake nor let [you] down (relax My hold on you)! [Assuredly not!]"(emphasis mine)

Now that you realize that you are not alone and God walks with you through every minute of your life, take your time in selecting friends. Find friends who share the same interests, perhaps the same major as you. Make sure you have friends that share the same values, beliefs and faith as you. Most important of all, remember that you have a friend for life. Proverbs 18:24b "…there is a friend who sticks closer than a brother." (Amplified Bible) God says He will never leave you or forsake you and He is a friend who sticks closer than a brother. You are never alone!

The Writing on the Wall

So whether you eat or drink, or whatever you do, do it all for the glory of God. 1 Corinthians 10:31 KJV

Though more than forty years have passed, I remember the occasion like it was yesterday. Cheerful sunshine ushered in my first day of college in early June. Rose gardens on campus perfumed the air, and it seemed God had painted the landscape every shade of green on my college campus in the Missouri Ozarks. Even the high-pitched song of the goldfinches welcomed me. Everything about the day felt perfect.

I experienced a kaleidoscope of emotion when Dad, Mom, and my younger sister drove away, leaving me to embark on this new chapter in my life. Feelings of excitement and anticipation danced in my brain. I had looked forward to this day for a long time.

Amidst the zeal for new adventure, however, questions bombarded my thoughts. Will I make new friends? Where should I go to church? What will I choose as a major? Uncertainties threatened my peaceful anticipation. "Show me what to do, Lord," I silently prayed.

As the dinner hour approached, I found my way to the dining hall. Standing in line I met my first new friend. Janet and I shared a common faith in God and sensed an immediate camaraderie. "Thank you, Jesus," I whispered.

While eating our meal, I spotted a large banner painted on one wall of the room. The words of 1 Corinthians 10:31 were elegantly scripted, "So whether you eat or drink, or whatever you do, do it all for the glory of God." That verse became the theme of my college years. When worry and anxiety attempted to overwhelm me, I'd remember, in whatever I do, I can't go wrong if I do it all for the glory of God.

Like a Dog in a Pickup Truck

See to it that no one takes you captive through hollow and deceptive
philosophy, which depends on human tradition and the basic principles of
this world rather than on Christ. Colossians 2:8 NIV

I was on my two-mile walk the other morning when I witnessed something that caused a double-take. A pickup truck sped past me when a dog literally rolled out of the back of the vehicle and landed on the road! Fortunately the driver saw it too and immediately stopped the truck. A young boy rushed out of the passenger side to retrieve the dog. After a brief examination, the dog appeared to be unharmed and the boy led him into the safety of the cab. I couldn't tell how it happened, but my guess is that the dog was enjoying the breeze and got too close to the edge.

The edge…

Whether in art, music, clothing, or just lifestyle, it's quite in vogue these days (and perhaps no place more than on a college campus), to be on the edge. It connotes excitement, danger, thrills. It's seeing how close you come to the match before getting burnt. How near to the boundaries without actually stepping over the line. How far the rules can be bent without breaking them. Those who deem coolness the measure of all things especially gravitate to the edge, because whatever else the edge might be, it's regarded as cool.

The draw to adventure resides in every human heart. None of us desire to live in a bland black and white world. Pop culture promises a kind of glory from living on the edge but it's a promise it can't keep. Don't fall for a cheap substitute when you have access to the real thing.

Life certainly exists beyond the boundaries of the church. We all know we're called to be "in the world" but not "of it." At the same time we are cautioned not to test the Lord. "So, if you think you are standing firm, be careful that you don't fall!" (1 Corinthians 10:12). History is strewn with those who thought they were standing firm but ventured too close to edge and were swept away. Don't be one of them. Don't let your college experience thrust you over the edge.

Don't end up like that dog in the pickup truck.

Be Careful What You Taste

Taste and see that the Lord is good; blessed is the man who takes refuge in him. Psalm 34:8 NIV

Steve, a young newsboy stopped at the home of a customer. The man asked him if he liked honey. Steve wasn't fond of honey, but to be polite, he told the man that he would take a taste.

The customer went into another room and returned, carrying a small jar of honey. Upon giving it to Phil, he said, "That will be twenty-five cents." The boy sadly dug deep into his pockets and handed over a quarter, which was his entire allowance for the week. He thought his customer was offering a free taste of honey, but instead he was asked to purchase something for which he had no desire.

At times Christians may be tempted to take a taste of something that God forbids. Perhaps a movie or something on the Internet attracts their interest, but after watching and listening, they feel unclean, as though their minds have been polluted with garbage. Then they realize they've given something of value for a thing that was worthless.

Perhaps a family was torn apart because of an act of adultery. One mate believed another person would better suit his or her needs and desires, and so they deserted their spouse and family for a taste of forbidden fruit.

A fatal accident may have occurred because a drunken driver chose the taste of alcohol over sobriety. A young mind may have been damaged because of an addiction to drugs. These things happened because someone willingly allowed themselves to be tempted to taste of the wrong things.

The opening scripture tells us: "O taste and see that the Lord is good; blessed is the man that takes refuge in him." After we have tasted what God has to offer, we may find ourselves hungering and thirsting for more of his goodness. Temptations to sin will lose their allure.

Unlike Steve, who was asked to pay for the honey before he could taste it, God's salvation and goodness are offered without charge to those who will accept it.

In the Grip of God

O LORD, you have searched me and you know me. Psalm 139:1 NIV

There are times when loneliness overpowers, causing doubt and fear to find us. It is comforting to remember God is always with us. His love and warmth wrap us in a gigantic hug if we allow it. There are times we find ourselves in the midst of strangers and unfamiliar surroundings. Before long these new things will become old and comfortable. They will be the stability we seek.

A few years ago I found myself alone, in a new home, a different state; and thrust into a life I was not prepared to embrace. Change became my middle name. However the one thing that had not changed was my God. I learned early on God never changes; I can count on His Word to be my stabilizing factor.

Change can be good. It can offer fresh opportunity; a chance to do-over or do-different. Once I allowed myself to relax and embrace it, this season of life change turned into an adventure. God sees what we need and He will provide. His timing is perfect.

Consider how your dorm room is different from the room you left behind. The change is significant. It reflects who you are becoming; a young adult on the verge of tomorrow. Tomorrow conveys a different future.

If I rise on the wings of the dawn, if I settle on the far side of the sea,
even there your hand will guide me, your right hand will hold me fast.
Psalm 139:9-10 NIV

The beginning of college life is like facing a new dawn. The horizon is no longer recognizable, but the stunning color takes ones breath away. The road before you is not yet mapped out, the path not yet worn down and some twists and turns up ahead will require wisdom and direction to navigate. Allow God to guide you. Turn to the familiar unchanging words of Jesus for comfort.

It's A Different World

Congrats! You've graduated high school! You had a great four years. Easy classes, except for calculus and who has an easy time in calculus anyway; great teachers who were always willing to help you before and/or after school; good friends and lots of fun.

Now you are at college and the first thing you realize is you are in a different world. Nothing is the same as high school. Not. One. Thing.

First, instead of being in a room with 30 +/ – kids, there are 150 in your Philosophy course. Attendance was mandatory in high school; here it is optional. Your professor won't know if you are present or not—she has 149 other students to deal with. Of course, if you want to pass the class, I'd suggest you go to class. Your parents would appreciate it, too.

You show up for Philosophy the first day and long before the hour is up, you realize this is not your parents' philosophy. The stuff this woman is saying has nothing to do with the philosophy course you took in high school. She might as well be speaking Greek.

Next on your schedule is the ever-dreaded freshmen calculus. But you survived calculus in high school so this can't be that bad. Right? Wrong. It's worse.

Walking to your dorm, you realize you are in way over your head. No one told you college would be this difficult. No one told you that countless hours would be required just to keep your head above water in your classes. No one told you that you would be so overwhelmed on the first day that you would feel like you were in the middle of the Pacific, without a life jacket, going down for the third time.

Allow me to remind you of a couple of things. First, you are not the only one on campus that feels this way. I suspect that 99.99% of the freshmen class feels just like you do.

Second, and more important, you can do this. The Bible verse below says it all. God gives us the strength—"infuses strength in us,"—to do whatever we need to do. We are "self-sufficient in His sufficiency."

Don't give up. Pray daily, asking God for strength and help in your studies and in all aspects of your college life. He will answer your prayers!

I have strength for all things in Christ Who empowers me [I am ready for anything and equal to anything through Him Who infuses inner strength into me; I am self-sufficient in Christ's sufficiency.]
Philippians 4:13 Amplified

Life Happens With You

But the very hairs of your head are all numbered. Matthew 10:30 NKJV

Have you ever heard the saying, 'life happens while you are making other plans?'

Moving to college your excitement overflowed. You unpacked, thankful to finally be there. You met your roommate, who is just great but has her own group of friends. You walk to the cafeteria and you see hundreds of people walking, talking, and laughing—in pairs and in groups. You get your meal and look for a place to sit. The room is buzzing with excitement. You find a table in the corner. Your excitement slightly wanes. Homesickness lurks. Life feels like it is happening around you.

You feel alone but you are not alone. God is with you every step of the way. He knows you so well, down to your very last hair! He knows that entering a new place surrounded by new people can be daunting. Tell him your fears, your concerns. He will help you to make changes that will enhance your college experience.

Following these tips will provide you with immediate change.

- Reach Out—you are not the only person feeling alone. Sit with someone else who is sitting alone. When going to an event, ask another to join you. You may get a few 'no' answers but don't let that stop you!

- Attend Functions—being a room hermit is great for studies but does not make for a good social life. God provided families so that we have others to provide emotional support. Build your college 'family.' When you attend college functions, you open yourself to friendship opportunities, friendships that may stay with you your entire life!

- Join a Club—there are a number of organizations you can join through your college. Join one that is dedicated to something you are passionate about. Not only will you meet people you have something in common with, you will become more experienced and knowledgeable about your subject of interest.

Being alone is a temporary condition that is remedied by prayer and a little action on your part. Remember, you are never truly alone. God your Father loves you. He's proud of you for taking on a new challenge and will be there every step of the way while you make 'life happen' in your new environment!

Get Ready to be Surprised

Call to me and I will answer you and tell you great and unsearchable
things you do not know. Jeremiah 33:3 NIV

Doesn't a verse like this move you to the edge of your seat? Just knowing God wants to surprise and thrill me with "great and unsearchable things," humbles me and grabs my attention.

When I heard this the first time I knew God was saying something meant just for my ears. It is as if God were encouraging me by saying, "Stick with me, I have something so exciting to show you, you are never going to believe it!"

Right now there might be feelings of anticipation. Everything is new and different. For the first time in life we are on our own and feeling excited if not scared? So many things we are encountering appear surreal. But remember, God wants to show us amazing things. He wants to use us in amazing ways.

This is a time when we begin to live the life that is waiting for us, the life we have only dreamed. Perhaps the career path laid out, the one we are studying so hard to accomplish, is the dream of a lifetime. You too may sense God preparing you for such a time as this.

Live as though poised on the edge of your seat. Don't get comfortable or lazy, all curled up in the cozy over-stuffed chair. Be positioned for greatness. Isn't that what living for Jesus is about? Now is not the time for fear of the unknown, it is time for the assurances we have in Jesus.

When I find I am caught up in an uncomfortable situation, I recognize it is time I turn to God for direction. When there are more questions than answers, there is only one thing to do. Turn it over to God and do the next right thing. His ways are mysterious and what was a puzzle today just falls into place tomorrow.

What does the picture look like once all the pieces are in their rightful place? Use your imagination, call on God and expect him to tell you great and unsearchable things you do not know. You won't be disappointed.

Wise Choices

*Now it happened as they went that He entered a certain village; and a
certain woman named Martha welcomed Him into her house. And she had
a sister called Mary, who also sat at Jesus' feet and heard His word. But
Martha was distracted with much serving, and she approached Him
and said, "Lord, do you not care that my sister has left me to serve alone?
Therefore tell her to help me." And Jesus answered and said to her, "Martha,
Martha, you are worried and troubled about many things. But one thing is
needed, and Mary has chosen that good part, which will not be taken away
from her. Luke 10:38-42 NKJV*

I have always wanted to do more things than I was capable of doing.
If there was a job to be done, I would volunteer for it, especially when
it came to working in the church.

As a pastor's wife, I enthusiastically took on playing the piano,
teaching a Sunday school class, working in the women's ministries,
helping with youth groups, and visiting the sick, all while raising four
children and serving my husband. I enjoyed the activities, and felt I
was pleasing the Lord in the things that I did. But sometimes I felt
overburdened with too much work.

One day while I was praying about my busy schedule, I complained,
"Lord, I don't know how I'm going to get all these things done." Quietly,
He spoke into my heart, "My child, have I asked you to do all of these
things?"

It is important that we ask the Lord what He wants us to do about
an offer, a choice, or a situation, yet we need to remind ourselves that
what we do is not as important as who we are. As the saying goes, 'We
are human beings, not human doings.' The Lord will lead us, if we let
Him. Let us always remember to choose the good part, sitting at His
feet, so we can make wise choices.

Decisions, Decisions

I face them every day. Some I give little thought to, but others I make only after great deliberation.

My life has been filled with decisions. Enough to fill a book. Many of them minor, but quite a few major. I decided to get out of bed this morning and go to work. I could have kept sleeping, but I would have had to call in and tell a lie in the process. I would have lost one of my vacation days and possibly my job if the truth was discovered. A somewhat minor decision, but one that could have negative repercussions.

Moses had some tough decisions as well. He was leading a cantankerous group of people through the wilderness toward the Promised Land, but there was no end to their complaining. Then Moses cried out to the Lord, "What should I do with these people? They are ready to stone me!" Exodus 17:4 NLT.

The question I ask myself is, "What do I base my decisions on?" Do I base them on my emotions? If so, I'm in trouble. God created all of my emotions, so they are healthy in and of themselves. But they are also very fickle and change regularly and rapidly. One occurrence can take me from happy to angry.

I can also make decisions based on my interests. This may be acceptable if my interests are aligned with God's plan for my life at a particular time. Otherwise, interest-based decisions can take me down paths of disobedience. Since I constantly do battle with my fleshly nature, this can happen very easily.

So what should I base my decisions on? Prayer, the principles of God's Word, and the direction of his Spirit. Are you allowing God to help you make the major as well as the minor decisions of life?

Prayer: Eternal Father, may our decisions be made only after we've consulted You.

An Understanding Ear

Jesus Wept. John 11:35 NIV

I felt hurt. Hurt that my trust had been abused. Would I ever be able to trust that friend and confidant again? Who would I share my pain with? My sorrow? My failures?

Confidence in a friend is sometimes all that we have when life throws chaos. Struggles can send even the most secure person into an emotional tunnel of darkness. Our first reaction is often to reach out to our bestie, our BFF. The person to whom we tell all of our secrets. The person who knows us best. But what happens when that trust is broken? Who do we turn to when the one we trusted most in our lives has broken a confidence or just doesn't understand?

In these two simple words – Jesus wept; we learn everything we need to know about our Creator. In these two powerful words, Jesus shows us a God who cares deeply and understands profoundly. He lived as we live, struggled as we struggle.

Life in Bible times wasn't much different than it is now. They gained and lost friends, fell in love, lost people they cared about, were seduced by material things and desired to be known and treasured. The same as us. Different scenery; same struggles. They experienced much of the same emotional ups and downs as we do. I imagine that there might even have been a friend or two that fell for the same guy – sound familiar?

Emotional highs and lows weren't restricted to just the completely human either, Jesus often expressed deep emotion which messed with the traditional thought of the day – the Greek concept of an emotionless and detached God. He has felt every emotion that we have felt. He understands the struggles that we have and the desire to share them with someone who understands.

Some of the deep emotions that Jesus showed were compassion, indignation, sorrow and frustration. Have you ever felt any of these? Are there things that you feel inside that you could never tell a friend? Turn to Him with your questions, your pain, and your sorrows. Honesty can always be given; there is no judgment, only love, kindness and guidance that you can trust.

Share your hurts with someone who understands. Someone who has felt it all. And who will never fail you.

Jesus has an understanding ear.

Put On Your Track Shoes

Therefore, since we are surrounded by such a great cloud of witnesses, let us throw off everything that hinders and the sin that so easily entangles, and let us run with perseverance the race marked out for us. Hebrews 12:1 NIV

"Blend in by standing out," the speaker at my grandson's high school graduation ceremony advocated to the four hundred capped and gowned teenagers. Those students have probably forgotten these words by now, but for this grandmother they were jewels of wisdom.

Good advice, to be sure, even in today's secular world, but perhaps even better advice for college Christians to follow.

"You are so nice." "What makes you so different?" "You're so caring about everyone." These statements often come from unbelievers to those inside the Christian circle who display desirable qualities. Likewise, "they're no better than the rest of us" is said by these same people when they see behavior unbecoming to followers of Jesus.

Athletic or not, each one of us is running a race in the arena of life, being watched by a large crowd of spectators. Unlike other races, this race isn't about finishing first; it is ongoing for the rest of one's life. May those watching you from the sidelines see you blending in with the crowd but still standing out because of your desirable differences. Know that your cheering section is rooting for you and be assured that victory is certain!

You are His Home

Do you not know your body is a temple of the Holy Spirit within you, which you have from God? You are not your own; you were bought with a price. So glorify God in your body. 1 Corinthians 6:19-20 RSV

This verse hit me between the eyes as a teenager, because I had never believed that our bodies are as important to God as our minds. I viewed the body as a 'lesser' part of me, or as 'unclean' in some way.

I realized that I had unconsciously picked up the teaching of our age which comes from the ancient Greek philosophers – that the mind is superior to the body; therefore we should honor the intellect and suppress the physical.

The Bible challenges that. The view God showed the Jews, is that the person is a whole being, body mind and spirit, and each part is equally important.

So if our body is God's temple, and the Holy Spirit lives in us, then we are his home! We are a 'holy' place. If God dwells in me, I want to make the best home for God that I can. Keeping a moderate level of fitness, getting enough sleep to not be a 'grumpy temple,' eating well. (Sort of – I was a teenager!) I also chose not to smoke or binge drink.

My work as a physical therapist made it even more real to me: my body, the temple of God, is the instrument He uses to care for others and bring healing. My work, when I touch people and treat them, is a conduit of God's love and power. This blew me away. It still does.

Best of all, it changed my attitude to myself. Some of us have come from a background where we do not see our bodies as special to God. We look in the mirror and think, "Yuk!" Maybe we have not treated our own body well by taking drugs. Or maybe we have come from a past where we have been physically or verbally abused.

When you became a Christian, God's Spirit came to live in you. Jesus died to cleanse you from sin – mind, spirit and body. No longer are you 'unclean,' but you are holy. You are His home.

High School Relationships

The Lord is close to the brokenhearted and saves those who are crushed in spirit. Psalm 34:18 NIV

Boyfriends, girlfriends, friends, and family. It's all going to be different when you head off to college.

It's a fact of life: people change when they go to college. You get to be more independent and you get to meet all sorts of different people. Be careful not to hang on to your high school relationships so tightly that you can't truly experience what God has for you in college.

When I started college, I was still dating my high school boyfriend. We had been together for almost two years, so we figured my starting at the university across town while he finished high school wouldn't be a big deal. The problem was, though, that I spent all my time with him. I missed him and I hung out with him and I went to his football games. I skipped out on a lot of college stuff for those first few months because he was the only thing on my mind. Plus, I got a little jealous when he wanted to just hang out with his high school friends. One thing led to another and our relationship ended. I was utterly heartbroken and missed out on more college adventures for at least another month after that because I was still hung up on the situation.

One of the cool parts about college is you get to take on the world on your own and just learn about yourself. Get closer to God and figure out who He wants you to be during those four years. Don't let a high school relationship get in the way of that, if that's not what God has for you during your college years. Now I'm not saying it's absolutely impossible to keep your high school relationship and friendships in college, but it is going to be very different. Just pray about it and ask God to keep the important people in your life. If someone needs to leave your side, ask Him for the strength to be okay with that. I know it will hurt, but God will always be your friend.

Mood-Driven or Mission-Driven

Have you ever had great intentions and then got in the way of yourself? Had a true vision and plan but then did something lesser, something else? This often happens to me. My flesh and feelings can be my enemy when I have a goal I want to meet. Humbly examining this tendency further, I realized I needed some kind of bottom line biblical wisdom. The Lord reminded me that I need to be mission-driven, not mood-driven.

Philippians 3:12 says, "Not that I have already obtained all this, or have already been made perfect, but I press on." (NIV) So, despite emotions, I must press on, regardless of feelings or responding to the enemy who seeks to discourage and destroy me. Next time I make a choice, I need to ask, "Is this move mission-driven or mood-driven?"

For example, let's say my mission is to be a good steward of my one and only God-given body. I know this honors Him and can see the value, but, on a disappointing day, suddenly comfort food is tempting! Being mission-driven, I can realize purpose trumps pleasure and could stay true to my course. (As opposed to being mood-driven and a pint of Death by Chocolate disappears from the freezer!)

The same thought process can be used with money (the mission being to save and give and tithe as opposed to an emotional spending spree) and the list continues indefinitely.

Granted, this is often easier said than done. There will always be some mood-driven moments in our humanness, but surely we will be better for every time we pick mission over mood. Let's exercise mission muscles instead of mood muscles! Thankfully, the Lord will be with us each step of the way, giving His strength and encouragement and grace. How true is Hebrews 13:20-22! "May the God of peace...that great Shepherd of the sheep, equip you with everything good for doing His will and may He work in us what is pleasing to Him. Amen!" (NIV)

Not Alone

A time is coming and in fact has come when you will be scattered, each to your own home. You will leave me all alone. Yet I am not alone, for my Father is with me. John 16:32 NIV

As I meandered through the nearly deserted student union, I could have said those very words. Cornell University was on a mid-semester break. The break period was too short to justify taking the Greyhound bus all the way home to Maine and back, but long enough for all my classmates to head home to their families.

I was alone. Feeling small.

Have you ever felt that way? Sometimes we even feel alone in a crowd, if we're surrounded by strangers. That includes people who know us but treat us like strangers. Being different, blocked from the inner circle of friends—that's enough to make anyone feel alone and small.

But we can say, as Jesus did, I am not alone, for my Father is with me. We're always right at home, in the biggest and best family circle: our Father God's embracing love.

Bridging the Cultural Gap

The LORD, before whom I have walked, will send his angel with you and prosper your way. Genesis 24:40 ESV

I sat in the College and Career Group at church in my first year of university thinking, 'I don't belong here.' The young city people were strangers and seemed so sophisticated, wise in the ways of the world. Although I had been looking forward to university, I hadn't anticipated being so uncomfortable in a church.

Although I didn't have a word for it, I was experiencing culture shock, the disruption and disorientation when one is suddenly placed in an unfamiliar way of life or culture. I went to university a shy farm girl, with little experience in the wider world. In addition, I was very unsure of myself. The gap between being well known in my small church at home and being a stranger in a large church seemed an insurmountable chasm.

I didn't see it then, but God gave me a solution to help ease me into city church life. I decided to attend a church across the city which my sister and her husband attended. It was a smaller church, with other people I knew. And because bus service was irregular on Sunday mornings, friends living nearby agreed to give me a ride.

Over the years I would see how God gently led me in small steps as I discovered a confident adult identity. These years of maturity prepared me for greater culture shock when I lived in South America and faced a greater cultural difference.

God knows that university and college can be a time of great abrupt changes and transition. Sometimes we can't leap over the chasm to adjustment all at once, so God sends his angel to lead us across the bridge, guiding us with his comfort and strength as we catch sight of the raging river below. But God also knows that that on the other side great opportunities await us.

Thank you, Father, for your faithfulness in taking us through the many unknowns of university or college. Thank you that you are with me, and will give me your presence, love and direction. In Jesus' Name, I pray, Amen.

The Collision

Twenty-two percent! It was my first exam at university. My professor of Canadian-American history had posted the marks on his door in descending order of excellence, identifying us only by our ID number. In anticipation I began scanning the ID numbers, starting at the top. I looked down to 50%. My mark wasn't there. My alarm grew as I found it. 22%.

I privately faced the disgrace of a 22% exam, too embarrassed to tell anyone. What escaped me was that the exam had been marked severely. Other marks were below mine.

This was the nadir of my first year of university. While I no longer remember the content or form of the exam, nor the professor's comments afterwards, I knew I had to do something different.

I had valued excelling in my education. Although I had worked hard in high school to become the valedictorian, something had not prepared me for university.

My present and past education collided.

I had to make changes in the way I studied. I needed to absorb information from lectures. I needed to write better essays presenting my opinions and arguments. I was now required to use higher order thinking skills—synthesis and evaluation.

I was also not strong in my faith, but God Himself went before me. I found strength in Psalm 32:8. "I will instruct you and teach you in the way you should go; I will counsel you and watch over you."

While it took time to develop these skills, I eventually excelled, even receiving an award for the highest mark in one course.

When our past successes and current difficulties collide, when we face insurmountable situations, we can trust God to go before us, to send someone to encourage us, and to give us the discernment to make the necessary adjustments.

He will do it.

Father, thank you for what you have done in my life. Help me to know how to get the most out of my studies and to excel. Where I am successful, help me be an encouragement to other students who are struggling. In Jesus' name I pray, Amen.

A Gift from God

Jesus used the scriptures in His life. After His forty day fast in the wilderness, He defeated the devil by quoting scripture and standing upon God's Word (Matthew 4:11). Our finite thoughts often confuse and throw a shadow on the wisdom of God's truth. Even doubts, which Satan whispers to our mind, cause us to wonder at times. However, these are counteracted by the comfort, direction, rebuke, instruction and admonition, which we receive from the Bible (2 Timothy 3:16). We can trust in the absolute truth of God's Word. Even when we are not aware of it, God is working behind the scenes to prove to us the truth of His goodness and His faithfulness to His children.

The Bible is the perfect gift from God, which gives us everything we need to live a fulfilled life in a godly manner, through our knowledge of Jesus Christ (2 Peter 1:3). The Word of God is the sharp, two-edged sword of the Holy Spirit (Ephesians 6:17; 1 Thessalonians 2:13). The profound revelation of the nature and wisdom of God, written within its pages, builds our faith and guides us through life. All Scripture is inspired by God and is useful to teach us His truth (2 Peter 1:20-21). We can feed our body with the grain of the earth, but our spirit needs the nourishment that is found only in the Word of God (Matthew 4:4).

Prayer:

Lord Jesus, we stand upon Your Word. We use it as a lamp to light our way in this dark and dreary land in which we live. It gives us courage, peace and strength to do Your will with our life. We want to thank You for not leaving us alone on this earth, and for giving us Your Spirit and Your Word to encourage us and to give us hope.

Thought for the Day:

God's Word is alive; and the more you read it, the more it empowers your life

Living in an "i" World

We live in an "i" world. We communicate with our friends and family on our iPhones. When we do not have time to talk we can quickly iMessage while multitasking through other projects. We play games and make applications on our iPads. We do research and word process on our iMacs. We buy our music from the iTunes store so that we can listen to it on our iPods. It would seem that living in an iWorld makes everything about "i."

Paul writes in Philippians 2:3-5 (NAS), "Do nothing from selfishness or empty conceit, but with humility of mind regard one another as more important than yourselves; do not merely look out for your own personal interests, but also for the interests of others. Have this attitude in yourselves which was also in Christ Jesus." The challenge becomes in how we make choices to live within the context of a world dominated by "i" without be controlled by an attitude of "i." Consider changing your perspective as you transition from an inward "i" focus to an outward "i" focus by asking three "i" questions.

With whom do I have influence? Each and every day we find ourselves in unique groupings of people that are exclusive to us. Through conversations, mutual activities, and acts of kindness we interact with these people, which set a foundation of ongoing influence. Consistency of time spent together will allow for growth in relationship, which has the potential for developing contacts with the power to impact.

With whom can I make an impact? The easy answer to this question will come from the pool of people in which you have influence. So become intentional about being aware and alert to pursuing a small group of relationships that truly have the potential of accomplishing great things. Making an impact in the life of another will require removing your focus from "I" to "U." This will take time and effort but when this happens you will now be able to discern how to answer the next question.

With whom can I invest? When you make an investment you are expecting a return, so choose wisely. You can have influence with many and impact several but you can only successfully invest in a few. Jesus influenced thousands, impacted hundreds, and invested in twelve. And they changed the world. Begin today living in a new iWorld!

My Three-letter Word Promise

In addition to all this, take up the shield of faith, with which you can extinguish all the flaming arrows of the evil one. Ephesians 6:16 NIV

I had to read the verse twice to make sure I'd understood it correctly. ALL the flaming arrows of the evil one. The passage did say ALL, didn't it? I read it for the third time. Yes, ALL. What a wonderful one-word promise to claim in time of anxiety. With the shield of faith we can extinguish ALL the flaming arrows of the evil one.

College students face trials that can be real joy stealers. Meeting impossible deadlines and dealing with disagreeable people challenge the strongest among us. Add to that, the ache of being away from home for the first time, and life, at times, can feel overwhelming.

Our enemy, the devil, attacks us from every angle. When faced with new struggles, he tempts us to sin by planting seeds of doubt and confusion in our minds. We don't have to give in to the turmoil, though. The Word of God tells us to take up our shield of faith when Satan sends those fiery arrows our way. Spending time in the Word of God and in prayer raises our shield. As we put our trust in God and rely on his power to defend us, we are able to avert the lying schemes of the enemy.

I am grateful for this passage of scripture and the hope conveyed through one three-letter word, ALL. Not some . . . not most . . . but ALL.

Precious Father, thank you for the shield of faith, which can extinguish ALL the flaming arrows of the evil one. Teach me to use your weapons with power and effectiveness. In Jesus' name. Amen

Looking Sharp

People look at the outward appearance, but the LORD looks at the heart.
I Samuel 16:7b NIV

Approaching my car in the parking lot, I couldn't help but admire the sleek, shiny bodywork. It's not an especially new vehicle, but I'd recently washed it and felt quite classy as I unlocked the door and slipped into the driver's seat. Shifting gears into reverse, I checked my mirrors, then turned to look through the rear window—and caught sight of the back seat.

Any sense of 'glamour queen' crashed into the reality of 'parent of young child.' Despite my cleaning efforts, a trip the previous afternoon had yielded a scatter of paraphernalia across the back seat. No matter how good the car's exterior looked, anyone who glimpsed inside would have seen the nest of pens and paper, scribbly drawings, sand (yes, sand!) and other odd items.

I believe it's important to have a healthy relationship with our body: self-respect by dressing well, maintaining good hygiene, fitness and health. But if our outer expression becomes our identity, it's like my flawed confidence in my car's outward cleanliness. We can become so focused on our 'look' that we forget the more important maintenance of our inner self.

The reality is that if we're a tumbling mess inside, no style facade will hide it. As soon as someone gets close enough to peer through the 'window,' they will see the true condition of our heart, which will also reflect in our actions. Just the same, when we look at others it can be easy to judge by their appearance and in so doing miss the brokenness that may be underpinning a fashion statement or behavior.

We need to care for our inner self—our spirit and soul. A key to this is found in the words of King David. "Search me, God, and know my heart; test me and know my anxious thoughts." Psalm 139:23 (NIV) Our God is the healer of broken hearts (Psalm 147:3). If we let Him search and renew the deepest reaches of our heart, He will bring a contagious vibrancy to our lives, outshining even the most finely polished surface—from the inside out.

When Love Fails

*Love is patient, love is kind. It does not envy, it does not boast, it is not proud.
It does not dishonor others, it is not self-seeking, it is not easily angered, it keeps
no record of wrongs. Love does not delight in evil but rejoices with the truth. It
always protects, always trusts, always hopes, always perseveres. Love never fails.*
1 Corinthians 13:4-8 NIV

As children, we are surrounded by love. Like a warm blanket it wraps
its arms around us, protecting our hearts with something we did not earn –
unconditional love. The love of our parents is our first real taste of what God
feels for us. It's the knowledge that no matter what, we belong to Him and
that love can be trusted. It protects patiently, guides carefully and honors
sacrificially.

This concept of love is carried within our hearts into adulthood as an
example of what we should consider great love and worthy of our attention.
The friends we make, the people we date and our ultimate choice of a spouse,
are based on the love we received when young, and nothing is more devastating than when that love fails you.

We put our hearts fully into the hands of another, trusting that they will
care for it as our parents had; with the ultimate example of God's love and
care. But what happens when that trust is broken, stomped on or shattered? Is
this verse from Corinthians trustworthy in its message – love never fails?

The kind of love that Paul is talking about is an attribute of God. God's
love never fails. Human love? It is unreliable, yet potentially one of our greatest
qualities. But love is not just what you show your boyfriend or girlfriend. It
is not simply an emotion that we feel during times of happiness and contentment. It is so much more. Love is the expression of unselfish sacrifice, even
in the face of adversity and trials. It is made pure when we can give it, even
when it is not received. Love involves unselfish service and genuine concern for
another. But it is also respect; of others, but most often of ourselves.

This is how God loves us. Can we expect this kind of love from those
whom our paths cross? Possibly. But human love will almost always disappoint. It is only God's love that will not. It is His love that will hold us
together when we need it. To focus on Him and never lose sight of the love
that He has for us means that we will never be without perfect love. It is in
this realization that we find perfect peace and the happiness that will get us
through those times when the love of the world fails.

Wearing Masks

Be sober, be vigilant; because your adversary the devil walks about like a
roaring lion, seeking whom he may devour. 1 Peter 5:8 NKJV

I'm Ok, You're Ok was a resource used in my Psychology class. Its title
and classroom discussions left me with the impression that everyone's personal
philosophy was acceptable. As a young adult, I was turned off by the seeming
prejudices of older society. Uptight about so many things, their solution was
always another taboo. Whether strongly stated or in hushed circles, societal
norms were the sum of their thinking.

Ripe for the challenges of the future, I would embrace all people and
ideas with my open mind. I came to realize those views contradict the Biblical
message of vigilance. It's important to be alert amongst the masses. Often I
would stifle an uneasy feeling to make someone else feel accepted. In the end,
I always found they were NOT OKAY. Parental concerns weren't prejudices
after all, but insightful protection.

The Holy Spirit nudges us to be on guard for a reason. Evil is actively
seeking participation. It is prudent to establish core boundaries and pay attention to your instincts when they flare. We live in a day of school shootings and
campus victimization. Our response must be commensurate to that truth.
Open to new people, ideas, and adventure, yet alert to Masks.

Virginia Tech's mascot is a Turkey. Cherished by campus and community
alike, this bird can be seen in regal displays all around Blacksburg. I purchased
one as a keepsake. After careful inspection, I discovered my mascot was an
imposter. The turkey's head was a mask similar to a skullcap that could be
lifted off from the neck. It was really a bear in disguise.

At some point we all wear masks. Some protect like a welder's mask,
others conceal like a masquerade mask. Either way, be aware that people are
not always who or what they seem to be. Likewise, we should also evaluate the
masks we wear. There's a difference between being careful and being phony.
God created us to be unique and He loves His creation. Embrace your gifts
and talents as original designs. And walk your journey in the light of His
Word. It's supreme over all curriculum.

Remember, when the turkey was unmasked the real prize was a teddy
bear. How loveable is that?

We refuse to wear masks and play games. We don't maneuver and manipulate
behind the scenes. And we don't twist God's Word to suit ourselves. Rather, we
keep everything we do and say out in the open, the whole truth on display, so
that those who want to can see and judge for themselves in the presence of God.
2 Corinthians 4:2 Message

Friends Beyond the Books

Carry each other's burdens, and in this way you will fulfill the law of Christ. Galatians 6:2 NIV

I met Michelle during my junior year of college. Having been accepted as teaching candidates, we both felt the pressure of university expectations. Together we compared notes, studied for tests, and deepened our passion to teach. Our friendship was clearly a gift from the Lord. Yet, in those early days our bond had not yet been forged by the refining fires God allows all long-standing friends to experience.

The next summer brought a fight against the currents of depression as I said goodbye to a man I sensed was not God's best for me. Not long afterwards, Michelle called with strong resolve in her voice, "Come downtown with me. You need to have some fun."

Somewhat reluctantly, I forced myself to go along. By the end of the day, our simple outing had lifted my spirits. Through reaching out to me, Michelle boosted my faith in God's plan to see me through difficult trials.

Later that year, Michelle and I had Friday night plans to pick up a pizza. As I cruised along behind her in my little Ford Escort, I suddenly cringed when I watched her car collide into another vehicle. Quickly pulling over, I ran to stand beside my friend. Although Michelle was shaken, we rejoiced that both she and the other driver experienced no injuries. Later that evening, we read Romans 8:28 together, "And we know that in all things God works for the good of those who love him, who have been called according to his purpose."

As Christian students, we all aspire to achieve great goals for God's glory. We work hard to fulfill the requirements of our professors in order to graduate. Along the way God blesses our lives with friendships. These relationships deepen as we share the cup of suffering with one another. By carrying each other's burdens in Christ, we can rest assured we are fulfilling Christ's law for our lives.

Dear Lord, In the midst of all the tests, papers, and projects that we need to complete, let us not forget to make time for the friends you bring into our lives. Help us remember that by assisting others in their struggles, we bring you glory. In Jesus' name. Amen.

Our Ladders Matter

A ladder is something that can be used to get from one point to another. It is usually stationed at its base and its top leans or inclines toward something else.

The journey through college could be compared to climbing a ladder. It certainly involves moving from one point to another! A sobering proverb says this about ladders, "When you climb the ladder of success, be careful. You don't want to get to the top only to find you had it propped against the wrong building!"

College is a time of many choices. "Ladder leaning" opportunities are everywhere. What should I major in? Who should I make friends with? Where should I live? Who should I date? It would be easy to be swept under by the enormity of the many decisions college requires.

But there's good news. God cares about our ladders! Jacob, from the Old Testament, dreamed of a ladder. God was gracious enough to prop Jacobs's ladder right at the seat of His throne. We too can prop our ladders heavenward.

When we look to God for wisdom and discernment regarding life decisions we are leaning our ladders well. The climb up the rungs may still be hard. There are times, like Jacob, that we may wrestle. We may wrestle with ourselves or others. We may even wrestle with God. But a ladder leaned at the throne of heaven will always grant the climber peace.

Where is your ladder leaning?

Are you looking to God for help in the many decisions that come with college?

Ask Him for guidance in your decision making. Read his word and seek wise counsel. No one wants you to lean your ladder well more than God!

Barricade the road that goes nowhere, grace me with your clear revelation.
Psalm 119:29 Message

You're blessed when you stay on course, walking steadily on the road
revealed by God. Psalm 119:1 Message

I ask—ask the God of our Master, Jesus Christ, the God of glory—to make
you intelligent and discerning in knowing him personally, your eyes focused
and clear, so that you can see exactly what it is he is calling you to do.
Ephesians 1:17-18 Message

God's Cure for Worry

Has this semester gotten to you? Do concerns about keeping up have you down? Everyone has times of anxiety and stress, but has it turned into worry? Once worry becomes a problem, what can you do?

God has a cure. Take these action steps from God's Word in Philippians 4:6-9 (ESV).

Pray. *Do not worry….but….by prayer….let your requests be made known to God.*

You might feel you can't turn to God, because He might be too busy or you are afraid you can't trust Him. But you can. Talk things out with Him. He will listen because He cares. If you are angry, pray out loud. Yelling might even help. Just let Him know what you are thinking.

Procure Inner Peace. *And the peace of God, which surpasses all understanding, will guard your hearts and your minds in Christ Jesus.*

Your college courses will not miraculously turn around without a ton of hard work. So, make a list of what you can do as you think about this semester. What can lower your stress? Attend class more often? Develop better note taking skills? Make reading more your priority? Tutor for better test scores? What will guarantee a better semester?

I don't know of a better way to inner peace than to do all you can and then set it aside and trust the results to God.

Ponder the Positive. *Finally, beloved, whatever is true, whatever is honorable, whatever is just, whatever is pure, whatever is pleasing, whatever is commendable, if there is any excellence and if there is anything worthy of praise, think about these things.*

If you think the worst is going to happen then you will start to worry. If you take things into our own hands and don't trust God you will feel frustrated.

Worry thinks "God doesn't care and won't do anything, so I'll have to worry my way through this." Faith says "God cares. He and I will work it out together. I'll supply the willingness and He'll supply the power."

When you stay positive and keep praying, His inner peace will guard your heart and mind as you face your worries with His help.

How Am I Designed

I am the....life. John 14:6 NIV

Life matters.

We all want life to matter. We want to know the crescendo of our life will be worth having lived it. We want to be called to worthiness in life, but I'm not convinced that "calling" gets to the heart of what we mean to say and think. When we say "called" we're doing diligence to attack our jargon biblically, but I'm suggesting that doesn't peel back enough layers to reveal what we really mean or what God has actually done. God called out to Samuel, Jonah, David, so on and so on, but deeper than the calling was the design that fit them for the call.

We live designed lives.

I hear it often: "I'm called to do this," or "she's called to do that." I remember trying to make sense of this in my own life. Thinking God hadn't "called" me for anything. Terrified I would never figure it out, as if God finds pleasure in hiding it from me or dangling it overhead just out of reach. It wasn't until I stopped thinking in-terms of some spiritual epiphany, and began looking back over the design of my life, that it all began to make sense. Who had God made me to be?

I was designed, just like you.

Stop to reflect upon the threads God has woven into your life. Begin to see amazing patterns of design emerge. There are doors in front of you that only God could have opened. There are pains and joys unique to you. There are passions, gifts, and talents that you have. All these collide to create, you. Discover yourself again, and experience the joy of being who you were uniquely designed to be.

When Your Beliefs are Challenged

I tell you this so that no one may deceive you by fine-sounding arguments.
Colossians 2:4 NIV

College life is rich with diversity. It provides a great venue to get acquainted with different cultures, social climates and even religions. However, such vast exposure can prove challenging to your beliefs.

Some religions are more obvious in how they contradict Scripture; however, many religions have an element of truth which make them seem feasible and are, therefore, dangerous. In fact, these differences may even make more sense from a human standpoint. So, how can you tell what is true and what is counterfeit?

Study the Word

Cultural norms, fads, and new aged religious philosophies change ever day, but the Word of God is never-changing and is the anchor for our faith. Check everything you see, hear and read against it and if it isn't supported in Scripture, then don't give it any space to take root in your heart and life.

All Scripture is God-breathed and is useful for teaching, rebuking, correcting and training in righteousness, so that the servant of God may be thoroughly equipped for every good work. 2 Timothy 3:16-17 NIV

I love what the Apostle Paul told the church in Corinth in his second letter to them. He said, "We demolish arguments and every pretension that sets itself up against the knowledge of God, and we take captive every thought to make it obedient to Christ." 2 Corinthians 10:5 NIV

Pray for Wisdom

Ask God to help you not only understand and apply Scripture to the situation but also that you will know how to give an answer delivered with grace so the hearer will see Jesus in you.

If any of you lacks wisdom, you should ask God, who gives generously to all without finding fault, and it will be given to you. James 1:5 NIV

Seek Fellowship

Look for a group of like believers to hang out with. Most colleges and universities have campus ministries that meet on a weekly basis. Find out when these groups meet, check their doctrine and try them out. Some of the most popular groups are Cru, InterVarsity, and Navigators. Having an accountability group in college is a great way to stay on track with your faith and challenge growth toward maturity in Christ.

Enjoy the diversity! Just make sure stepping out doesn't mean stepping away from your faith.

Faith Leap

*The Lord makes firm the steps of the one who delights in him; though he
may stumble, he will not fall, for the Lord upholds him with his hand.
Psalm 37:23-24 NIV*

Life can take us on some wild adventures. My most recent adventure
felt like God was asking me to walk a narrow mountainside path to a
lookout and jump over the edge! 'Are you sure, God? There must another
way to go about this!'

Standing at the crossroads of decision can feel like that. Sometimes
when I ask God for direction, He seems to point me down a path that
looks like a dead end—and in that particular case, I was hard pressed
seeing much light through the undergrowth. Yet, something I've learned
about those dead ends is that when He calls and we respond in obedience, He's always faithful to meet us on our way.

There are many voices that call to us in these decision making
times, offering advice, telling us what's best. Yet, I realized that often
the greatest voice I had to contend with was my own.

Doubt. Little seeds can grow big roots—especially alongside craggy
mountainous paths. Even when I knew unquestionably that I'd made the
right choice—which meant probable job loss—in the natural it seemed
like career suicide. I'd find myself fretting. Had I heard wrong? Did I
misunderstand? This can apply to many areas of life. We need to learn
to trust the voice and wisdom of God and let Him have control, even
when in the natural we can't quite figure it out.

I look back now with the benefit of hindsight and nearly roll my
eyes at myself. Oh, what a plan God had in store! But I didn't know
that at the time. I just knew He had confirmed what I needed to do
and (somewhat tentatively) took that leap. Sometimes opportunities
don't look like we expect them to. Sometimes the journey involves a few
bumps and diversions. But obedience to the call of a loving Heavenly
Father will always open the way for His provision.

Lord, thank You for guiding our steps and giving us confidence to
know that when we respond obediently to your call, You will open doors
of opportunity and furnish our journey with overwhelming provision,
down to the finest detail.

Remember Who You Are

*Therefore if anyone is in Christ, he is a new creature; the old things passed
away; behold, new things have come. 2 Corinthians 5:17*

If college is about anything, it is about change. New classes. New
instructors. New room. New food. New friends. If it seems as though
everything in your life is different suddenly, there's a simple explanation:
it probably is.

However, for the believer in college, it is almost guaranteed that in
the midst of this whir of "different," there will be a very real attempt by
the enemy and those hostile to the cause of Christ to get you to abandon
what is "old." Your old way of life before college when you walked
confidently in your faith is often somehow painted as weak-minded and
naïve. You will most likely be challenged to question everything you've
ever been taught, have believed, and have lived since you were saved.

Statistics tell us that for some, this assault is so intense and the
questions so unrelenting that they will waiver, first questioning and
ultimately leaving the faith altogether. Reputable data suggests that for
every ten students who attend church in high school, anywhere from six
to nine will stop going to church for at least a year during college, and
four out of ten stop going forever beginning during the college years.
These are students who were raised in Christian homes, participated
in Christian ministry and missions projects, and regularly sat under
Biblical preaching and teaching—sometimes for nearly their entire life.
And in less than two or three years, all that is cast aside.

As a Christian, the thought that we could be so easily swayed is
scary. As a parent, the thought that my child could be so easily led
astray is as devastating as it is terrifying.

So how can you hang on to a faith that has been so core to your
identity during your younger years when it seems like everyone around
you is turning their back on God?

Be like a lion.

In Disney's *The Lion King*, young Simba finds himself in a rut
contemplating his purpose in life. He is idling along, pretty much
doing nothing of consequence other than eating, sleeping, drinking,
and hanging with his friends.

Sound familiar?

That's when an encounter with his father, the king, challenges him and changes him forever.

"Remember who you are."

Did you get that? Remember. Who. YOU. Are.

No matter your testimony or your history, if you are a believer, you are not the same person you were before salvation. You are a new creation. In 2 Cor 5:17, God's word tells us that you are a new creation and that the old you has passed away.

If you were blessed enough to have been raised in church, you probably have a long list of ministers, teachers, volunteers, and other folks who have poured into you. God called you and you answered. The King, your Father, desperately wants you to remember who you are.

So many young believers find themselves in the midst of temptation and fall for the lies, and just like Simba, they have settled for far less than service to the king. They are more than they have become.

So in the moments when the pressure to conform seem too much and it seems like everyone else is falling away, stand firm. Stay the course. Reaffirm in your mind regularly—day-by-day or even moment-by-moment if need be—that you have been called and prepared for a purpose.

You are a new creation. The old life IS gone. Your new life IS come. And it need not change even though it seems like everything else in your world already has.

Remember it.

Come Out From Hiding

By day the Lord went ahead of them in a pillar of cloud to guide them on their way and by night a pillar of fire, so that they could travel by day or night. Exodus 13:21 NIV

I learned early on that I didn't have a gift for languages. The discovery came in my first year of college when I had to take a foreign language as a requirement. I chose Italian.

I can still see myself poring over vocabulary lists in my dormitory room, listening to auditory prompts in the language lab, translating texts at my desk with an Italian dictionary close by.

But soon it became clear that my personal study wouldn't be enough. I still had to participate in class. And that was another story.

The fact was that I struggled in the classroom. I froze with fear I'd make a mistake in pronunciation, grammar, or translation. I hoped against hope the instructor wouldn't call on me. I shrunk down hoping to become invisible.

Before long I floundered and fell behind. Yet I couldn't afford to fail the class. I finally made an appointment with my instructor to talk about how I could improve my grade.

Once in his office, I nervously stated my case. Kindly, he listened. Then he spoke words I've never forgotten.

"Miss Black," he said, his eyes locked on mine. "You'll never learn anything as long as you hide behind the person in front of you."

Fear. It freezes us. It stops us from growing. It causes us to create smoke screens to hide behind. Sometimes it's the fear of trying something new—like learning a foreign language. Other times it's the fear of standing up for our beliefs or reaching out to help someone.

But the good news is that we don't have to be afraid. We have no need to hide behind something (or someone!) like an imaginary pillar. We have a guide. Our guide is the same pillar that led the Israelites and provided light for their way—our Lord Jesus. He will help us out of our fears, give us direction, open a way through any difficulty. Strength and courage come from him each day, day and night.

Pillars are not for hiding behind. The True Pillar is the One to follow.

Find Your Elizabeth

*Trust in the Lord with all your heart, and do not lean on your own
understanding. In all your ways acknowledge Him, and He will make your
paths straight. Proverbs 3:5-6 NASB*

It can be discouraging trying to develop your path in life. Much
more so when people you love, whose opinions you respect, discourage
you from trying to achieve what you know God has called you to do.

Imagine how Mary must have felt. An angel appears to her and
tells her she will conceive a child as a virgin. She is excited! An angel
personally and audibly told her, and encouraged her saying, "For nothing
will be impossible with God" (Luke 1:37). And, yes, she told other
people. Her fiancée broke up with her. Her friends probably scoffed at
her, and laughed behind her back. I shiver to think what her parents
and family said. So a brokenhearted and threatened Mary fled her home
and sought comfort with her relative Elizabeth.

Elizabeth received Mary with open arms and cried, "Blessed are
you among women" (Luke 1:42). Elizabeth believed what the Lord had
spoken to Mary, and encouraged her.

How often are we discouraged when we share the innermost secret
of our heart with someone? How often do their words hurt us and
convince us not to try what God has called us to do?

It is important for us to listen to what the Lord speaks to us, and
act upon it. It is equally important that we find someone we respect
who will encourage us and pray for us as we embark upon the path the
Lord has set before us.

It isn't hard to find people to tell us we can't do it, that we aren't
qualified. But God doesn't call the anointed, He anoints the called.
He won't take you on a path that He hasn't already prepared the way
before you.

Surround yourself with people that will wrap their arms around
you and encourage you saying, "Blessed are you." "You can do all things
through Christ Jesus who strengthens you" (Philippians 4:13). "For
the Lord will be your confidence and will keep your foot from being
caught" (Proverbs 3:26).

And when God puts a dream in your heart, answer Him as Mary
did, "May it be done to me according to your word" (Luke 1:38).

English 101: Pass or Fail

Trust God from the bottom of your heart; don't try to figure out everything on your own. Listen for God's voice in everything you do, everywhere you go; he's the one who will keep you on track. Proverbs 3:5–6 Message

Who would have thought Billy Graham could help me pass English 101?

After graduating at the top of my class (okay, it was a small high school), I got a rude awakening at a university where class sizes exceeded my entire senior class. Rumor had it that freshman English courses were used to weed students from college. Getting a D– on my first paper made me wonder if I'd pass or fail.

I needed a course correction—fast. Fortunately, the teaching assistant offered pointers to improve my writing.

The next assignment was to write a paper to convince. Mostly, I needed to convince the teacher, and maybe even myself, that I could write. I chose a topic I felt passionate about: Billy Graham. I'd heard him speak and admired his courage and faith.

After long hours of researching at the university library, I gathered my copious notes to begin writing. With lots of prayer, I completed my convincing argument and turned it in.

When it was time to retrieve my paper, I wasn't sure I wanted to see the grade. But one look told me they weren't rid of me yet. I had gone from a D– to an A+!

My introduction to college wasn't unique. Most college students face challenges and difficult classes. But these challenges will prepare them for the future, if they stay the course and trust God—one assignment and one course at a time.

I received a C in English 101 that quarter. But four years later, I graduated cum laude. "Billy Graham" was my only A+ in college. One day I'd like to thank him for his help.

College courses were training ground for future writing. I went on to publish hundreds of articles, columns, and a book. I still apply what I learned in college—completing one assignment at a time with God's help. You can too.

Heavenly Father, thank You for these exciting and challenging college years. Help me trust You fully and listen to Your voice. I know You're the only One who can keep me on track and help me pass. I choose to lean on You. In Jesus' name. Amen.

Cry Out in Faith

They were helped when they cried out in battle. 1 Chronicles 5:20a NIV

David was a young shepherd who was chosen to be the king over Israel (1 Samuel 16:13). Yet we also know that by the time he was being called out, he had watched over herds of sheep that were attacked by lions and bears. He had had his fair share of troubles and would face many more throughout his life.

Even still, David is called a man after God's own heart (Acts 13:22). Regardless of his mistakes and suffering, David again and again turned to God and cried out for help (Psalm 31).

Don't assume that because you are in battle God doesn't care for you. Sometimes we must battle. There is a false belief that if God is for you, life will be easy. Don't believe this lie.

Our faith in the Lord does not promise us an easy life, but does provide the tools to handle whatever we face.

In 1 Chronicles the Israelites were in battle. In the midst of this battle, they cried out to God and he heard them and helped them, "because they trusted in him." 1 Chronicles 5:20b NIV

Think of the trust required in battle to cry out for help from someone you can't see. Imagine the faith that requires!

Some of you are in battle or will find yourself in battle shortly. Attacked and weary – cry out in faith! Trust that God will hear you when you cry out to him.

Be encouraged by David's words "Be strong and take heart, all you who hope in the Lord." Psalm 31:24 NIV

Prepared in Advance

While I slept this morning, my automatic coffee maker made coffee and my automatic bread machine made cranberry bread. When my alarm automatically went off at the right time, I got up to enjoy the automatically made coffee and bread, while reading an automatic electronically delivered devotion.

It may have seemed automatic this morning, but that's only because of all the preparation the night before. Looking only at the morning's events, you would assume life was easy. Just get up, pour some coffee, and eat a hot, ready-for-you breakfast. But it's not that simple. The preparation the night before took effort.

That's the hard part for me. Knowing how and when to prepare, and putting forth the effort to do something with the hope and confidence of a future benefit. Any fool can pick a tomato. It takes someone with a lot more foresight and action to plant the tomato plant three months earlier.

It might be nice to be the guy who is always prepared, but I am not that guy. Sometimes I miss the chance. Sometimes I don't see what's coming. Sometimes, when I am very tired or very busy, I don't do what needs to be done to be prepared for tomorrow. In those times especially, I realize I am not in control. I can't prepare for everything. Even if I had the energy and willpower, I don't have the foresight. But there is One who does.

Perhaps at times we face situations where we are unprepared so that we learn to rely more on the One who is always prepared. He knows the future and He is willing to direct our paths if we listen and follow. He is never surprised; always prepared for what is ahead. He is preparing a place for us in Heaven, and I think there's a good chance He's preparing some places for us on Earth too. Places we may be next year, or next month, next week, tomorrow . . . or this afternoon.

We should always use wisdom and good judgment, paired with courage and willpower to act in preparation for the future. But if on occasion we should happen to arrive at a place in life for which we feel totally unprepared, we should look up and take comfort from God who, long before we arrived, was already there, prepared and waiting for us.

The LORD your God, who goes before you, He will fight for you, according to all He did for you in Egypt before your eyes, and in the wilderness where you saw how the LORD your God carried you, as a man carries his son, in all the way that you went until you came to this place.
Deuteronomy 1:30-31 NKJV

Trials into Triumphs

It is better to trust the Lord than to put confidence in men. It is better to take refuge in Him than in the mightiest king! Psalm 118:8-9 LB

I buried myself under my covers, shaking in fear. Worry over the unknown factors of life filled my soul with endless stress and debilitating fear. I constantly sat on the edge of my seat, holding my breath, fearing some potential catastrophe that probably would never happen. I methodically attempted to control every aspect of my life, in order to keep myself safe. I did not want to relinquish all of my cares to God, fearful that He would not take care of me.

As I prayed about my fear, God reminded me that at the moment I recognize anxious thoughts disturbing my soul, I could remember that God ultimatly turned every one of my past trials into blessings for me and that nothing could ever separate me from His love (Romans 8:35-39). As we watch God turn our trials into triumphs, we actually lose our fear of the future and start looking for the seed of His miracle within each hardship we face.

Our lifeline during negative circumstances comes from remembering that our enemies and negative circumstances will never triumph over us (Psalm 25:2). Our sufficiency is from God alone (2 Corinthians 3:5-6). We can breathe deeply from the depths of our being with the assurance that all of our circumstances work out for our ultimate good (Romans 8:28). Relying on God is better than depending on the most powerful person in the world! (Psalm 20:7).

Prayer:

Lord Jesus, the next time I get between a rock and a hard place, remind me not to be discouraged or upset. Help my unbelief and give me the courage to expect You to act in my defense (Mark 9:24). We have plenty of reasons to praise You for all that You do and will do for us. You are our God. You are our help (Psalm 42:11). I will put my trust in You today and always.

Fear not, because God is with you. Isaiah 41:10.

Finding Time for Bible Study

All scripture is given by inspiration of God, and is profitable for doctrine,
for reproof, for correction, for instruction in righteousness.
2 Timothy 3:16-17 NKJV

A man once told D.L. Moody that he planned on getting just enough from the revival to last his entire life. D.L. Moody told the man that doing what he said was like eating enough breakfast in one sitting to last a lifetime. We both know that this is an impossible feat to do, but sadly some Christians are doing just that.

Just like we have time to make ourselves physical beautiful or to fill our stomachs, we need to also nourish our soul. To do this, we need to daily find time to read our Bibles, pray, and spend time with fellow believers.

As a college student, I know how hard it is to find time to spend time with God. I struggled to find enough time with all of the work I had to do to read the Bible. I eventually found myself too busy to read God's word. One night, I was working on a devotional and felt like a huge hypocrite. Here I was trying to help others and I wasn't doing what I was supposed to be doing. But the conviction was clear and I needed to change. I prayed that night asking God to help me spend more time with him. I realize now that I was not only short changing my spiritual growth, but more importantly my communion with God.

Now everyday, I make it a regular habit of reading the bible because I know that it can help deepen my understanding of God and help me grow closer to Him. Growing spiritually is a life-long process that takes time.

Dear Heavenly Father,

Please help us to not neglect our time together. And when we read your word give us a deeper understanding and wisdom. Help us to be still and know that you are God so we can hear your voice.

I pray in Jesus' name.

Amen.

Perfectly Imperfect

God arms me with strength and He makes my way perfect.
Psalm 18:32 NLT

Sometimes I wish I could be perfect. I am a first-born. It comes with the territory.

Dr. Kevin Leman, the author of *The Birth Order Book*, describes a first-born as being goal-oriented, self-reliant and a perfectionist. He says, "First-borns prefer to know what's happening and when. They thrive on being in control, on time and organized."

Oh, yes, I'm a first-born.

Wanting to get everything right and feeling frustrated when I can't are issues I am learning to recognize are a part of my thinking. I can be hard on myself when I feel like I don't measure up to the standards I've set or those others expect of me. When I try to be perfect I always fail.

While the desire to be perfect is a natural part of my personality I've learned that I am not defined by my perfectionism. It shouldn't have a hold on me because God loves me as I am and I can be released from trying to make myself perfect.

I am in a loving relationship with Jesus. The value He places on me defines who I really am. He does not expect me to be perfect in order to love me. He gave His life for me because I am imperfect and sinful. His love for me is unconditional.

Being a perfectionist is not limited to first-borns. You may struggle with perfectionism like I do, even if you are the second-born, third-born, or baby of the family. Here is a promise I found in God's Word that helps me trust Him with this whole perfectionism issue. Maybe it will help you, too.

"The God of all grace [Who imparts all blessing and favor] …will Himself complete and make you what you ought to be, establish and ground you securely, and strengthen, and settle you." (1 Peter 5:10 Amplified)

No matter where we are in our family's birth order we can stop trying to make ourselves perfect. What we can do is let God be in charge of developing us into who He created us to be, a person who is whole and complete in Him.

We are Chosen

For he chose us in him before the creation of the world to be holy and blameless in his sight. In love he predestined us to be adopted as his sons through Jesus Christ, in accordance with his pleasure and will — to the praise of his glorious grace, which he has freely given us in the One he loves.
Ephesians 1:4-6 NIV

I grinned when I saw the return address on the letter. It was from the missions agency. Two months earlier I had applied to serve as a summer missionary through my Christian student association. I was certain God wanted me to spend my summer serving him overseas. I ripped open the envelope, eager to see my assignment.

My assignment wasn't in the envelope. I stared numbly at the words. Thank you for applying. . . unfortunately we didn't have the right assignment for you this year. . . praying for you as you plan your summer. I was shocked. I searched the letter for answers, but didn't find them. My mind began to supply my own list of reasons:

Rejected

Failure

Not good enough

Unwanted

Rejection stings. When we don't get the job, lose the scholarship, don't make the team, or are passed over for the fraternity or sorority of our dreams, it hurts. In those moments of rejection we are tempted to accept the labels others put on us. Nerd. Stupid. Slow. Lazy. Annoying. Unwanted. Unloved. But other's acceptance or rejection of us does not change our identity. God determines our identity. The labels that matter are the ones he gives us.

Ephesians 1:4 tells us that we are precious to God. Others may reject us, but God chose us before the foundation of the world. Before the world was made, God saw us. He saw our weaknesses and our failures. He saw the things that would make us stumble, the times we would reject him, and the time others would reject us. He knew us. And he chose us anyway. We belong to him. Our destinies are not determined by fate or chance, but by a loving God who chose us and gave us a hope and a future. He chose us to be holy and blameless before him, knowing that the price paid for our acceptance would be the blood of Jesus. In Christ we are chosen as sons and daughters of God. When others reject you, take comfort in this: Christ has chosen you for his own. You are accepted in him.

Comparisons

*Let us fix our eyes on Jesus, the author and perfecter of our faith, who for
the joy set before him endured the cross, scorning its shame, and sat down at
the right hand of the throne of God.*
Hebrews 12:2 NIV

Compared to her, I feel so small.

My stature's short, and she is tall.

She's a leader. He's a brain.

Her words are dazzling, mine are plain.

He's an athlete, and wins the praise.

She'll be a beauty, all her days.

And then, there's me, just plain old me.

But I'll be the best that I can be.

In the race of life, I'll win the prize,

If I always keep Jesus before my eyes.

Housewife No Longer Desperate

*I denied myself nothing my eyes desired; I refused my heart no pleasure.
When I surveyed all that my hands had done and what I had toiled to
achieve, everything was meaningless, a chasing after the wind: nothing was
gained under the sun. Ecclesiastes 2:10-11 NIV*

*Many are the plans in the mind of a man, but it is the purpose of the Lord
that will stand. Proverbs 19:21 ESV*

As I sit here in my apron and house slippers with bread baking in the oven, I think back to days when I was desperate to find my future mate.

I always had a plan. Married with kids before 30. I got to a point during college where I was not concerned with anything except finding my partner. The person who would "complete me." Instead of focusing on my studies, I invested every moment of free time into my relationships with guys, all the wrong kinds. I somehow always picked men who claimed to be Christians but had a blatant disregard for any sort of biblical principles. I no longer cared whether these young men were actual Christians or not because of my plan. And I found myself in a world of hurt.

My grades were slipping and I nearly got kicked out of my parents' home. I tried to mold myself into someone who could hold on to my boyfriend. I became nothing more than a party girl. I found myself not even caring that I was pushing my own family away. And as far as God's plan for me, it no longer mattered. I was in relationship after relationship just grasping for one that would lead to marriage. I felt so completely alone even though I had a boyfriend and a huge group of people I partied with every single weekend.

I hit rock bottom, and when I looked around, all of the people I had made such a priority in life were completely gone. I felt like I had no one. My parents and family would have been there for me had I shared my feelings with them, but I was too ashamed of the life I had chosen to live.

That is exactly what Satan wants for you. He wants to isolate you and ruin your physical and spiritual life. But the second you let go of your plans and reach out to Jesus, He is there. I began attending a campus church group called Chi Alpha. There I met a young woman there named Amma. She was older than me, she wasn't married, but she was in love. Amma loved Jesus so much that His presence surrounded me when I was near her. I began to share with Amma how I felt so lonely, and she gave me a book called Falling in Love with Jesus by Dee Brestin and Kathy Troccoli. I am not much of a reader, but I read this book in 24 hours. It was incredible! It showed me that Jesus is the love of my life. Only He can complete me and romance me like no other.

Once I let go of what I had been working for, God began to work in my life like I had never seen. To quote Christian author Tim Cool, I had been "too focused on the plan and not the Planner." A few years later, I met a young man at church and we were married. Even in marriage you will find yourself lonely if you do not cling to Jesus first and foremost. When you walk hand in hand with the Lord you are never alone. Even while trying to make things work my way, Jesus never did forsake me, and He never will.

I Make Myself Laugh

A joyful heart is good medicine, but a broken spirit dries up the bones.
Proverbs 17:22 NASB

In every situation, we have a choice: joy or misery. Sometimes, the choice is easy, and we are joyful. Other times are more difficult, and we have to choose to laugh when we don't feel like laughing.

Fortunately, joy is not a feeling but a gift from God. In John 14:15-17, Jesus says that if we love Him, we will keep His commandments and He will give us the Spirit to be our Helper to reside within us. In John 15:11 He says "that My joy may be in you, and that your joy may be made full."

One morning I was cooking breakfast for my family before we began the day. I was really grouchy and nagged at them until they were grouchy and bickering, too. I was stirring eggs at the stove in my fuzzy house shoes, stained robe, and crazy hair, when I realized, "I did this. I put the whole family in a bad mood." And I wondered, "If I created this tension, could I also create happiness?"

So I started to laugh. I laughed out loud, louder and louder. I bent over laughing and slapped my leg. I even snorted a time or two! My children looked at me in shock. Then they glanced nervously at each other and back to me. Soon they were chuckling. Then they were out and out laughing. Oh, I know. They were laughing at me, not necessarily with me. But the point is, they were genuinely laughing, and left for school happy and content.

I learned on that day that His joy lives within us and wants to help us be joyful, no matter what we are feeling. We just need to tap into Him. Two things have helped me to do this: focus the mind, and make myself laugh.

I focus my mind on a happy thought: a time that made me laugh, a memory that always makes me smile. Then I physically laugh out loud. Sometimes this may begin like a strangled wheeze-like sob, but eventually it becomes a real laugh.

You, too, can call upon the Helper to help you, for as author Barbara Johnson says, "Pain is inevitable, but misery is optional. So stick a geranium in your hat and be happy!"

Run to God

Trust God from the bottom of your heart; Don't try to figure out everything on your own. Listen for GOD's voice in everything you do, everywhere you go; He's the one who will keep you on track. Don't assume that you know it all. Run to God! Run from evil! Proverbs 3:5-6 Message

Many new experiences grace the years one spends in higher education. Some of these come into your life for good, while others parade themselves in costumes of virtuosity, when in reality, they promote evil. If you don't arm yourself daily with God's Word, the evil one has an easier path to your mind. Even as Christians, we must keep our guard up.

This true story portrays how easily the devil can tempt us. Douglas and several of his friends decided to go to downtown Chicago for a night of dining and fun. Although against the rules of the Christian college they attended, they ordered wine with their meals. Douglas later said, "The minute I took the first taste, I knew this was what my body had been craving for years." The son of a well-known pastor in his denomination and the grandson of a General Superintendent, he had been raised in a home where no one had ever taken a drink of an alcoholic beverage. Doug became a severe alcoholic. He reached out for help, when he came to his senses. He discovered that two generations back a grandfather had been an alcoholic, but Doug had not been aware of that fact. One night's fun led him down a path which required years of rehabilitation, restitution, and repentance.

Did these students know better? Yes. Did they expect severe consequences? No. They did not get kicked out of college, simply because they did not get caught. But Doug's life started on a downward spiral that only counseling, rehab, and God's grace could mend. The devil tempts us at our weakest point and we can never be too careful.

So, as I Peter 5:8 in The Message reminds us: "Keep a cool head. Stay alert. The Devil is poised to pounce, and would like nothing better than to catch you napping. Keep your guard up."

Who Do You Say That I Am?

God calls us His masterpieces and promises to complete the good works He has begun in us. Do you believe this promise? Do you believe what God says about you? Or, do you believe what others say about you?

Gideon listened to voices other than God's (Judges 6-7). It not only affected how he saw himself but limited his ability to accomplish God's work. Gideon saw himself as weak and insignificant. He felt abandoned by God. He was no longer confident in God's promises that his ancestors had shared with him.

But God was able to see past Gideon's opinion of himself to whom Gideon could become. God called him a "mighty warrior." God called Gideon by the name by which he wanted Gideon to become. God reminded Gideon that He was with Gideon and in control.

Only God can provide you with the truth about who He created you to be. He knit you together. He knew you before time.

Seek God. Ask Him to show you how He sees you; how He created you. Keep asking until you see yourself as the masterpiece that God created. Then as Gideon did, respond in worship and move forward in confidence that you are fearfully and wonderfully made.

LORD, help me to see myself as the masterpiece you created. Continue to remind me until I see myself as you see me. Empower me to block out messages that don't align with who You say that I am.

Strength Training

God,

I never thought it would be so hard. This has been my dream to go to college, play ball, and earn my degree, but dorm life is crazy. I can't sleep, or think straight.

Everyone keeps telling me that this is the best time of my life. But do they know what it's like here? None of the brochures covered what goes on after classes end. The drinking, drugs, and carrying on right here in the dorms is out of control.

Last night campus police sat laughing and did nothing to stop a group of guys from carrying a drunken girl up the stairs. There are no boundaries, no one says, "don't do that" or asks "why" they just go along to get along, myself included.

Lord, how do I do what is right when everything around me is wrong? Talking to friends back home I act as if everything is fine. I don't want them or my folks to worry so I keep up the charade.

I admit that I haven't gone to church or sought out a Bible study since I arrived here. Every lifestyle choice, belief, and culture is accepted here, except Christianity and the last thing I want to do is stand out.

The few friends I have here don't believe in God. Lord, I am afraid to tell people what I think or believe. Everything about my life feels like a lie. I don't even know who I am or what I am doing any more.

How did you do it Lord? You were despised, cursed, and crucified and here I am hiding out. I am ashamed and angry for the way I am treating you.

Forgive me Lord. I know in my heart that you did not leave me.

Lord I need you! Guard my heart against the temptations I face and give me strength to stand for what is right. Lord I want to be the man you created me to be. I cling to your promise that you give strength to the weary and I am confident that you will see me through.

In Jesus' name. Amen.

So do not fear, for I am with you; do not be dismayed, for I am your God. I will strengthen you and help you; I will uphold you with my righteous right hand. Isaiah 41:10 NIV

The Right Road

If you wander off the road to the right or the left, you will hear his voice behind you saying, "Here is the road. Follow it." Isaiah 30:21 GNT

I was sure I was cut out to be a math major. Until, that is, I landed in the college infirmary and fell so far behind in my calculus grades that the math department "invited" me to find a different major. I felt humiliated and confused. Where *did* I belong?

A generation later, my son enrolled in a science major he'd eagerly planned. But he ran into difficulty and changed to English. After two semesters, he pulled another switcheroo back to science, putting him more than a year behind his former classmates. Where, I wondered, did *he* belong?

Though our changes of direction were rough at the time, I see in hindsight how the Lord guided each of us to the right road. My unplanned degree in psychology served me well in my career with a government agency. My son picked up useful skills during his English detour and returned to science with renewed focus, going on to obtain a graduate degree and a satisfying job as a lab manager. The Lord knew where we belonged and got us there, in spite of ourselves.

Struggling to find your "right" road? The Lord knows where he wants you to end up and the best—though maybe not the shortest or smoothest—route to get you there. Even if you take a wrong turn or two along the way, don't panic. The Lord can get you back on course. Pray for his guidance. Then listen for his voice saying, "Here is the road. Follow it."

The Purpose of a New Season

To everything there is a season. A time for every purpose under heaven.
Ecclesiastes 3:1 NKJV

My parents delighted me with the news that I would attend Michigan Christian College instead of a local college. Fairly sheltered, my excitement over my newfound independence was breathtaking. I visited home on occasion but not often. I loved my new living arrangement! I gave little thought to how my absence affected my parents and my siblings. The seasons of life brought me to that moment: a time when my life would have been much richer had I learned how to incorporate all the parts of me—my family, friends and church family—into my new life.

Nineteen years later I took the same journey my parents did. My son Brett prepared to leave my nest. Relieved at his choice and proud of him for moving forward, I didn't expect my strong reaction. Brett, his sister Natalie and I shared our final dinner as a single parent family after shopping for college essentials. Suddenly, the enormity and finality of the shift taking place in our family hit me. I choked back tears as I saw every moment I could have made better decisions, saw Brett's first day of kindergarten and realized that from this moment he was independent of me. Excited for his new adventure, I also felt the hole he was leaving. My perspective on going to college for the first time changed dramatically from when I was the one going to college.

As you move forward on your life journey know that you are appreciated; that you make a difference in the lives of your family members, your friends back home, and your church family. Pray for them, write to them, text them, call them, and find time to visit them. They will be delighted to hear about your exciting, new pursuits. Your journey will be richer for weaving the life you came from with the life you are developing. The purpose of this new season in your life is to build on what you are and where you came from. Your life will be richer when you take the time to weave in all the parts of you—past and present! Learning how to incorporate new experiences into your firm foundation is a lesson that will serve you well in any season of your life!

The Last Text

For God so loved the world that He gave his only begotten son that whoso-
ever believeth in Him shall not perish but have everlasting life.
John 3:16 KJV

"Where U At?"

Three little words that would be Sara's last. Texting and reading texts were what all of her busy teen friends did daily. How else could they be expected to always keep in touch?

She was driving home from picking up her new blue silk graduation cap and gown. The next day would have been high school graduation. She was so excited to be going off to college soon with some of her very best church friends.

All of a sudden, her cell phone rang and she looked down for just a few seconds to see the now unforgettable words of the text: "Where U AT."

They were to be her last text.

Her car careened into an unyielding cement divider wall and Sara went out into eternity.

If only she had left her cell phone in the glove compartment or trunk, she might be alive today.

But she had been so excited about her upcoming graduation that she seemed to lose all practical sense of the now.

The truth is that all of us will eventually read our 'last text.'

Whether it happens to be words heard, read, or said—our scheduled time will eventually come to meet our Master in eternity.

The Good News is that "whosoever believes in Him shall not perish, but have everlasting life." Sara had wisely made her confession of faith years ago. Thankfully she was now being ushered into the waiting warm arms of her Heavenly Father.

Some of Christ's last 'text' words on the cross to the repentant thief were: "Today you shall be with me in Paradise."

Just a few dramatic last words can make a lasting difference!

Prayer: Lord, thank you for preparing a home for me in Heaven. Amen.

Being Resourceful

The 'fish out of water' is a popular comedy movie formula. Sitting in comfy chairs, munching our popcorn, we laugh at the characters, as they bungle their way through their unfamiliar surroundings. All that they would normally rely on in their home culture with its technology, their family and friends has vanished. Amusing situations abound as they are forced to rely on their knowledge and past experiences. They have to become resourceful. Eventually in the movie, a way home opens up; a moment to step through the time warp, or to be transported through the cosmos. Then the movie ends.

But things are not so humorous when we are the fish out of water:

You have landed on the campus. Unfamiliar territory stretches out before you. The college buildings are spread out all over the landscape. You need a map, but you may be too embarrassed to use it. You wonder if you'll ever find your way around the place with any confidence.

The professors are strangers. There are hundreds, perhaps thousands of students on campus, but no one that you know. There are no friends and family other than the ones smiling at you in your photographs. You begin to feel utterly overwhelmed.

Like the characters in the movie, you need to look at the resources that you have with you. What resources did you bring other than your photographs? Among all those things you packed, you also brought with you the promises of God, and the purpose of a promise is to be claimed.

Where can I go from your Spirit?...If I rise on the wings of the dawn, if I settle on the far side of the sea, even there your hand will guide me, your right hand will hold me fast. Psalm 139:7, 9-10 NIV

Acknowledging such a promise can give you needed encouragement for each day, and you glorify God through the faith you have placed in Him. Encouragement is a valuable resource to have.

In fact, you walk each day with a God who knows the campus and its people very well. Jesus said to His disciples, and this is a promise for you today, *"Surely I am with you always, to the very end of the age."* (Matthew 28:20b NIV).

Remember Who is at your side to help you. Unpack and claim the promises of God and be encouraged!

Just Do It – Anyhow, Anyway

Therefore, since we are surrounded by so great a cloud of witnesses, let us also lay aside every weight and the sin that clings so closely, and let us run with perseverance the race that is set before us, looking to Jesus the pioneer and perfecter of our faith, who for the sake of the joy that was set before him endured the cross. Hebrews 12:1-2a

Having spent 24 years as the editor of a denominational mission magazine I know a little about deadlines. I was always faced with a deadline, just as you will be. At first glance, some deadlines seem a long way off. A report is due the first of March and it is now the first of January. Lots of time. Yes, but, if you begin now with a plan and organize the steps along the way, you will find that as the deadline draws nearer it is not as fearsome as you first thought. Plan, organize and set small, reachable goals.

One of the first things I learned was how to juggle. Today I have to work on the nearest deadline; I can also do a little work towards the next one; and the one farther down the road, well, I can make a phone call to set things in motion, borrow a book from the library; and see what the internet has to say about that subject.

My calendar was always a big help. I soon learned that there are 24 hours in a day, seven days in a week. What is due Monday could mean Monday at eight a.m. or Monday at midnight. What is due Friday at 5 p.m. may mean that nobody is going to look at it until Monday anyway. Don't be afraid to ask if you need to what the absolute deadline is.

I also learned two things that may seem contradictory: Don't leave it to God. But at the same time, put it into God's hands. The word impossible isn't in God's vocabulary. With God anything is possible; but it is also true that God helps those who help themselves. The most important thing is that you do your best to complete any assignment you have. More people fail in life because they don't try. Give it your best shot. It's the most anyone can ask!

He Understands

The phone rang and a chill raced through my spine. Caller ID confirmed my fear. It was him.

In frustrated confusion I answered. He was my boyfriend, so why was I so afraid? I should want to spend time with him, so why did I dread his voice? He was a good guy, or so everyone said, so why did he make me feel like dirt?

The guy was a youth pastor. Well liked in the community. A charmer. A man of God, studying to be a preacher. And he hurt me.

I was a brand new Christian. Logic says I was crazy to stay with the church. I was told it was my fault because I must have been dressed too scantily (a hoodie and oversized jeans?) or I must have been in the wrong place and the wrong time (he picked me up for dinner. I didn't know he had other plans…).

I decided I was okay with God as Father and God as Holy Spirit. But Jesus? Jesus, while fully God, was also fully man. And men were capable of hurting me.

My life verse at the time was Jonah 2:2: "In my distress I called to the LORD, and he answered me. From the depths of the grave I called for help, and you listened to my cry."

The Lord did listen to my cry. How can this Jesus truly be all-knowing, all-loving, all-present, and yet allow His people to experience such pain? I pondered this over tears and journal pages, reading endless books and pouring over the Gospels to find an answer.

Two years later, I drove away from college for a weekend trip to my parents' house. As I drove up the hill that served as the southern boundary to my college town, a song came on the radio – Jeremy Camp's "I know You Understand it All."

God touched me so deeply in that moment that I nearly had to pull over. He does understand it all. Jesus may not have been in my exact situation during His time on earth two thousand years ago, but He did experience just as much heartache. Crucifixion was a humiliating way to die. Not only that, but His accusers mocked Him, stripped Him naked, and divided up His clothes – His last remaining earthly possession. If our Lord endured all that, then I knew He could handle the pain of the assault I experienced my freshman year of college.

Jesus does understand it all. And as God, He hears our voice when we hurt and is fully able to handle our burdens.

Centerstage

Compared to the high privilege of knowing Christ Jesus as my Master, first-hand, everything I once thought I had going for me is insignificant – dog dung. I've dumped it all in the trash so that I could embrace Christ and be embraced by Him. Philippians 3:7-9 Message

Oh Jesus,
CenterStage of my life,
all my inner being
bounces the beat,
sways with the swing,
swoons with the croon
of the lovesong You sing;
stands to clap
in endless ovation
to the Glory that is You,
high-heaps bouquets of
adoration at Your feet,
raises its voice to belt out
with all the crush of saints
and angels here and above:
Glory! Hallelujah! High praise!
to Jesus,
CenterStage of my life.

Pennies from Heaven

And my God will meet all your needs according to the riches of his glory in Christ Jesus. Philippians 4:19 NIV

"Lord, how am I going to get a copy of the textbook I need?" I prayerfully fretted as I headed to serve breakfast in the student cafeteria. I tromped along through three inches of new snow worrying about the test scheduled for Monday.

The test would cover the professor's lectures and three chapters of the textbook. Due to tight finances, I had been unable to purchase the government book when winter quarter started. I put off purchasing it until payday from my cafeteria job. I had hoped that the first test in that class wouldn't be scheduled before I got my check but the once a month payday was still a week away.

"What am I going to do, Lord?" I asked. Though the book cost only ten dollars, that was an expensive book in 1968. With five other children to take care of, my parents were not able to help with my college expenses. Since the text was a newly chosen book, there weren't any less expensive, used copies available. The class was an evening class, filled with commuting students that I hadn't yet gotten to know so there wasn't anyone I could borrow the book from or ask to be my study buddy. Besides, since there weren't any Saturday classes, I didn't think any of the commuting students would be driving to campus that day in the snowstorm.

In fact, I didn't see anyone else out in the snow, but I did see something that indicated someone had been out and about. A ten-dollar bill was lying on the ground in the snow. In 1968 ten dollars was a lot of money. I looked around to see if someone was looking for it so I could return it; not only did I not see anyone, there didn't seem to be any footprints other than mine on the snow covered lawn. As I picked up the currency, I realized that it was more than provision for a textbook; it was proof that I could trust God's promise to provide. It was a promise I would depend on many times in the years ahead, and though the provision hasn't always been as dramatic as money in the snow, God is still keeping his promise to meet my needs.

A Good Place to Start

It is good for me to draw near to God. Psalm 7:28 NKJV

I prefer to hold my daily devotional time in the morning. If I wait until evening, after I have worked all day or run errands, I am not as alert or focused on this time with the Lord. Morning is the best time for me. But morning devotional time does not work for everyone. Parents are busy in the morning getting children off to school or feeding the baby. College students often have early classes leaving no time to slow down for devotions. Some people work the night shift so their "morning" is actually evening and that works best for them. Family devotional time can be the most difficult. Parents might have to be at work at different times. People who work two jobs find it even more difficult to slow down long enough to spend quiet time in God's Word and prayer. It does not take long each morning for the day to get busy and full. Time with God often takes a back seat to everything else on our schedule.

Fortunately, God is not limited by any schedule, calendar, or to-do list. He is always available. It does not matter what time of day or night we spend time with God in prayer and in His Word. It only matters that we do. As part of my devotional time, I read a chapter from Proverbs each morning. Conveniently, but not by accident, Proverbs has thirty-one chapters – a chapter for each day of each month. Though I have made this part of my devotional time for many years, I always find some new bit of wisdom or direction. Perhaps your favorite book is Psalms, Matthew, or Ephesians. It does not matter what book we choose to read. There is no book in the Bible that will not benefit us. It only matters that we open His Word and start reading. Jesus often went by Himself to spend time alone with His Father. We should follow His example. If you are struggling with finding time to spend in His presence, ask God to show you how to work this into your daily schedule. He will take it from there!

Draw near to God, and He will draw near to you. James 4:8 NKJV

Guaranteed Broken

When my friend Linda and I walked into Ollie's Bargain Barn, we spotted a sign: "Guaranteed Broken!" On the stand was an assortment of air conditioners. We asked a store employee if the sign was a mistake or a gimmick.

"No," she replied. "We guarantee they are all broken."

"Well, who wants them?" I asked.

"You'd be surprised. People buy them and repair them. Or they sell them to the scrapyard," the clerk answered.

I was in town for a graduation. I thought of the young people in yesterday's ceremony. Sitting on the field in their caps and gowns, they were on a high, convinced they could fix or deal with anything that came their way. Yet the commencement speaker reminded them that they would also face lows or brokenness.

He incorporated the nursery rhyme "Humpty Dumpty" into his address:

All the King's horses
And all the king's men
Couldn't put Humpty
Together again.

The speaker reminded the graduates not to be discouraged when they fail or break. He said it is only when we reach rock bottom that God can deal with the brokenness. It is only when we surrender our wills that God can repair us. Our God, unlike the king in the nursery rhyme, is capable of rebuilding broken people.

The commencement ceremony ended with communion where all were reminded that God gave His son to be broken for us so that we can be restored.

He healeth the broken in heart, and bindeth up their wounds.
Psalm147:3 KJV

Navigating Your Newfound Freedom

For my first year of college, I moved out of my parents' house and into a university dorm room three hours drive. Given the dimensions of this room, it felt more like a jail cell. On top of that, it wasn't even a private room! I had to share it with a guy I had never met. Fortunately, we hit it off well enough, and soon developed that friendship bond which is so important to sharing a jail-cell-sized room with another individual.

This was my first real taste of freedom: nobody telling me to do my homework, what to eat, when to go to bed. This was also a time in which I had to decide if the faith I claimed to profess was really my faith, or just an extension of my parents'. One passage of Scripture really stuck in my head during this time: Hebrews 11:24-25. This passage states that Moses chose to be aligned with the people of God, even if it meant he'd be unpopular, made fun of, mistreated, bullied, or worse. He'd rather face all of those things than to enjoy the pleasures of sin for a short time.

It's that last part that stuck with me – the pleasures of sin for a short time. In my first semester I was tempted with alcohol, experimenting with drugs, sex with very attractive suitors, cheating, even skipping out on church by placing attendance at Bedside Baptist. And I attended a Christian university!

All these seemed quite enticing; yet all the while, it was that verse, "the pleasures of sin for a short time," that stuck in my head. What would the pleasures, for example, of a one-night stand land me: parenthood before I was ready, an STD (27,397 university students in America contract an STD daily), shame – all for one night of meaningless pleasure. Thank God He kept that verse in my head!

That's when I realized what God meant in Philippians 2:12, "… work out your own salvation with fear and trembling." It meant asking God to be real in my life, to help navigate my newfound freedom. I asked God to prove Himself real to me during this time of newfound freedom, and He obliged. I encourage you to keep a journal of questions to God during your first year. Ask Him to prove real in your life, to help you navigate your newfound freedom. You'll be amazed at how He answers, and you'll be glad you kept a record of it.

Spoiler-Are You Alert?

*Now faith is confidence in what we hope for and assurance about what
we do not see. This is what the ancients were commended for. By faith we
understand the universe was formed at God's command, so that what is
seen was not made out of what was visible. Hebrews 11:1-3 NIV*

The Olympic season barely began and as a country we became fiercely
competitive. With every replay, gold medal finishes continually remind us
who the winners are. As the world watches, spoiler alerts are everywhere.

Even though we know who wins, we sometimes want to see exactly
how one runner overtakes another or how the team from pick-any-country
executed that perfect ice skating routine. But what about watching a
hockey game once you know the score? Most of us wouldn't.

Imagine: you watch anyway. The situation seems hopeless. Even
though you know who wins, you forget for a moment and get caught up in
how your team has fallen behind. Indeed, your team is losing 2-0 with five
minutes remaining in the third period. In the end your team wins 3-2....in
overtime.

You know how it will turn out because you have seen the end. But
life just does not work that way. All we see are tight deadlines and difficult
people and disappointments everywhere. Balancing school with family,
friends, and work takes all of our energy. We can't see where things are
going, we think we have lost and we feel lost.

Where we see deadlines, difficulties, and disappointments, we need to
remember that our God is the five-minutes-remaining-in-the-third-period
kind of God. It is in these tough times that our faith grows. Instead of
thinking we know how things are going to turn out and assuming others
are doing better than we are, lets take our faith into overtime by having
assurance about what we do not see (Hebrews 11:1).

So here's the spoiler: With Jesus as your Savior, God is eternally on
your side. Ask Him for more faith. Be the right kind of alert—alert to all
God is doing by remembering all that He has done. Only God knows the
final score. He brought you to this school, put you in the classes you are in,
gave you the friends you have—and He is not finished.

He created this amazing universe out of what could not be seen
(Hebrews 11:3). You are His most amazing creation. He loves you and
wants you to know Him more. If you want things to change, tell God. If
you feel like you don't have faith or you doubt He can do it, ask Him to
grow your faith. It is the third period...whom have you put your faith in?

To Whom Much is Given, Much Will Be Expected

From everyone who has been given much, much will be demanded; and
from the one who has been entrusted with much, much more will be asked.
Luke 12:48 NIV

The Crisis Hot Line was a free program available to everyone in the community. A church close to my college campus donated the office space. Volunteers were encouraged to share God's word with those who called for help. I knew I was young, about to graduate from college. Could I help? I also knew I was given much in life: I was blessed with a family who loved me and guided me towards many blessings. As a psychology major, this work at the Crisis Hot Line fit my life's goals. I knew much would be demanded from me, and I had some trepidation. I also trusted that if God asked me to help someone, the right words would come at the right time.

My first call was from a middle-aged mother who wanted to end her life. She said she was sad because her children did not need her anymore. I prayerfully listened and knew this call was directed to me from God. I understood from the side of the child. When I was 10, I found my mother sick because she had purposely taken too much medicine. Help came soon, and we both grew to know that we were blessed to have each other. I prayed, "Dear Lord, please use my experience to give me the right words to convince this mother that she will always be important to her children." I asked her if her children ever ask her to do any shopping. "Oh, yes. My daughter always wants something new. I can't always afford it, but I try to get something nice most of the time." I asked her if anyone else ever does this for her children. She laughed. "Oh, no." Then there was a pause. "Yes, I will always need to be here with my children. Even when I am sad." At that moment, the mother agreed to get evaluated by her doctor. I never knew for sure if she did, but I was confident that both of us realized we had been given much. Now, we both knew we had much to give. We said a prayer of thanksgiving to God. I knew that my studies and my faith prepared me for my life's work.

Awesome Place

When Jacob awoke from his sleep, he thought, "Surely the LORD is in this place, and I was not aware of it....How awesome is this place! This is none other than the house of God." Genesis 28:16,17 NIV

Runaway Jacob was on his way to find his Uncle Laban, seeking refuge from the justifiable anger of his brother Esau. At a certain place he stopped at sundown, grabbed a rock for a pillow, lay down and promptly fell asleep. And what a dream he had! There was a stairway reaching from heaven to earth with angels of God ascending and descending. Suddenly the LORD Himself stood there, reaffirming to Jacob the covenant He had made with his grandfather Abraham, concluding with the promise: "I will not leave you until I have done what I have promised you." (Gen 28:15)

When Jacob awoke he was awestruck. Last night this just looked like a good spot to make camp—but now it had become "an awesome place!" because his awareness was opened to realize that the LORD was there too!

By faith will I recognize that *wherever* I am, the LORD is there too? And He makes any place "an awesome place" by His presence.

...because God has said, 'Never will I leave you; never will I forsake you.' Hebrews 13:5b NIV

He Knows the Plans

*For I know the plans I have for you, declares the Lord, plans to prosper you
and not to harm you, plans to give you hope and a future.*
Jeremiah 29:10-12 NIV

If you had a special pair of binoculars that could look into the
future what would you want to see?

Some of you may want to know who you will marry, what you'll
be doing after you graduate, and if you will be successful in a career.
Others may not care about things so far away. Maybe you would like
to know if you will pass a certain course and get a decent grade, or if
you will have enough money to pay for next semester.

Not knowing what will happen in the future can be the cause of a
lot of stress for us. We might be thinking 'If I only knew that everything
was going to go the way I want it to, I could relax and I wouldn't have
to worry. Then I could start enjoying my life knowing that it is all going
to work out in the end.'

Unfortunately, only God is omniscient, knowing and seeing everything in the past, present and future. Nothing is hidden from His sight
and that allows Him to know exactly what is going to happen to us.
Not only does He know what is going to happen in our future, but He
has planned what is going to happen.

He is asking us to trust Him. He wants us to trust Him with the
plans He has already made for us. He knows how to make those plans
fall into place. Plus, He has good things planned that we will actually
enjoy. What could be better than the hope that this brings!

Jesus Meets Our Needs

Blessed are those who hunger and thirst for righteousness, for they will be filled. Matthew 5:6 NIV

On the dry African savannah a drought had stretched on for months. The land was parched and the people were hungry. The gardens were withered, the cattle gaunt.

Where we lived, nestled between two villages, our rain tanks were dry and any drops of rain were a blessing. We were all praying for rain desperately... Everyone's livelihood depended on it.

People only ate what their small plot of land produced. There were no supermarkets or grocery stores.

One afternoon a cloudy sky broke forth and rain dropped from heaven; big heavy, pounding rain.

We could hear children outside their huts giggling and yelling as they splashed in the mud as we listened to the rain pummel our tin roof and fill our tanks.

In chapter five of the book of Matthew we learn how Jesus spoke to a large crowed and taught them that those who hunger and thirst for righteousness will be filled. This is a promise we can cling to.

Do you know what it is to really hunger and thirst for righteousness?

Our hearts are like a dry land desperate for water without fellowship with the Lord. Jesus gives us the example to follow that even he regularly took time by himself in prayer.

As the deer pants for streams of water, so my soul pants for you, my God. Psalm 42:1 NIV

Our hearts are in desperate need of Jesus. Without him they are dried deserts where no growth occurs. When we realize this, then we can come nearer to knowing the joy that comes from knowing Jesus as He meets our every need.

Downshifting in to "Granny Gear"

He will also keep you firm to the end, so that you will be blameless on the day of our Lord Jesus Christ. 1 Corinthians 1:8 NIV

I once thought pedaling a bike up an entire mountain to be appallingly unappealing. Setting aside my misguided belief, I joined a small posse of nonconformists to clip the cleats of my shoes in to pedals and spin thousands of cycles upward.

As I advanced on the climb it wasn't long before my heart felt as if it would explode.

I shifted to granny gear. You know, the gear in which your grandmother could climb a steep hill. On this day, I was thrilled to have this mechanical advantage on my bike. I could reduce the stress on my circulatory system and press on to reach the summit.

When the pressures of success and the cravings of your soul entice you to seek notoriety, consumerism and pleasure over authentic fellowship with God remember that you can shift in to granny gear.

Do these steps seem like something you could do?

- Start by recognizing His altogether otherness.
- Move toward worshipping Him because He is worthy of worship.
- Surrender your self-sufficiency and self-importance to His divine nature and eternal power.
- Trust Him to work out all things for good according to His perfect will.
- Believe with assurance He will show up – not in your way, or your timing, but in the way God knows is best.

True greatness is realized in the drudgery of the commonplace. Every spin comes under the influence of God. On the trail I am met with roots, rocks, hairpin turns along with the strain of smooth uphill climbing.

You don't have to be a super hero disciple of Jesus on the trails of life to come to maturity. It is better to be committed to piecing together a series of tiny pedal strokes of faith. Just keep pedaling.

Your life and character formulate godliness when you seek and search for God not only to defeat fear and transcend adversity but in the ordinary. Over time you will be able to reflect on the many mountains you've summited.

Leaving Home

"For I know the plans I have for you," declares the Lord, "plans to prosper you and not to harm you, plans to give you a hope and a future."
Jeremiah 29:11 NIV

I was happily settled. I was involved in a great church. I was surrounded by family and friends. My sister had recently announced her pregnancy and I was eagerly anticipating being an aunt. I had a job where I enjoyed the work and the people. Life was good and I was content.

Unexpectedly, I began to feel unsettled. I often read a newspaper published in a city two hours drive from home. One day I noticed a job advertisement. A company was looking for someone with experience to fill a vacancy in my field of expertise. I felt God whisper, "This is your job." My reaction was surprise and excitement, mixed with hesitancy. I sent my application and soon received a letter offering an interview. This was an exciting time but also a challenging one. A time of anticipating change in every area of my life. I nervously headed off to the interview.

The next evening, I received a phone call from the interviewer – the position was mine and they wanted me to start within two weeks. Reality hit, bringing with it tears and nervousness, as I realized I had to uproot and relocate to a new place, with new people, a new job, a new church. New everything! I felt so ill-prepared for this big move. But, I knew without a doubt that I had heard from God, and that this was part of his plan for my life. So amongst many tears and much heartache, I obediently packed up my belongings, said my goodbyes, and moved.

The outcome? I am happily married to a wonderful man. We have two beautiful children. I have many lovely friends. We are involved in a great church. I enjoyed my job until I resigned to be a mum. I continue to grow in God and as a person. Was it difficult to follow God's leading and relocate? Yes. Was it difficult to leave behind all that was familiar? Yes. Was it difficult to step out in faith believing that the Lord would go before me, and that He had a good plan in all the change? Yes. Was it worth following and obeying Him? Yes! Absolutely yes!

New Beginnings

Whatever is true, whatever is noble, whatever is right, whatever is pure, whatever is lovely, whatever is admirable—if anything is excellent or praiseworthy—think about such things. Philippians 4:8 NIV

Mistakes. We've all made them, but instead of dwelling on what we did wrong or what we didn't accomplish, let's look ahead. Concentrating on our failures wastes valuable time and brings us down. I've been there, done that, and sometimes still do it.

Focusing on reasonable resolutions is a better choice. Setting impossible goals just adds more stress to our lives. The Bible says, "The thing you should want most is God's kingdom and doing what God wants. Then all these other things you need will be given to you." Matthew 6:33 (The New Century Version)

Instead of making haphazard lists of many of the same things we never accomplish, let's find a secluded spot, away from the TV and noise of the world, and spend time with God before making a new list. By seeking His guidance, that's how we will discover His purpose and plan for us.

Remember, God is not looking for extraordinary people; He is looking for ordinary people like you and me through whom He can do extraordinary things. We just need to be open to His will for our lives so that He can be gloried through us.

Thirty years ago, God opened new doors for me when I turned fifty. I never dreamed I'd be writing poetry and devotions and getting published. But I can assure you that by following His will, my life is more exciting and rewarding than I ever dreamed possible.

God wants to do the same for you. Take Him up on it. You'll discover that His unique plan for your life is better than you ever imagined.

Set Free

His power is made perfect in our weakness. 2 Corinthians 12:9 NIV

Diabetes. Confirmed. I can't repeat the first word that came to mind. For years I'd battled weight gain, and lost.

I wasn't a fat child, just slightly padded. A bout of mumps at age fourteen helped me shed a few pounds which prompted me to diet. By the time I was sixteen, my boyfriend could stretch his hands around my waist and touch finger tips. I was chuffed! I limited my energy intake to 500 calories a day for months before my body decided I was starving it. My metabolism rebelled – a 'hormone imbalance' they called it then. I packed on the pounds. Now I had Diabetes.

My doctor said, "I'll refer you to a Diabetes Educator for dietary advice. Get some exercise. Walking is good."

I replied, "I was an anorexic teenager. I'll have to summon that willpower again."

"No," he said. "You need to guard against developing an eating disorder."

Eating disorder! I went home despondent. I prayed, "Lord, help me lose weight," but I thought, *I need the anorexic me back again.*

I hauled the treadmill out of storage and began to pump. My thoughts drifted to the story of the Gadarene demoniac. The incident puzzled me. Why did Jesus allow the Legion of demons to enter that herd of pigs? As I pumped, I pondered…

That Gadarene was strong. No-one could subdue him. He had willpower. But wait – his strength came from the demons that controlled him. Jesus set the Gadarene free, but he permitted the demons to enter the pigs. (Luke 8:26-39)

The metaphor was not lost on me, even if the association with obesity is unfair to pigs. By seeking that anorexic willpower, was I simply giving my *demons* a second chance? Those strong demons drove the pigs to their destruction! Did I want an eating disorder strengthening me? Controlling me? Driving me? Or did I want to be free?

I prayed again, "Lord, set me free from eating disorders, that I may dwell in my right mind and proclaim the great things you have done for me."

I maintain a balanced diet and a healthy weight range now. I do so with God's help, not flawed willpower. Are you struggling with an issue? Need willpower? Release? Ask Jesus for his help. Why? His power is made perfect in our weakness (2 Corinthians 12:9).

Finding a Lifelong Friend

Joan found the perfect birthday card
two little girls in plaid dresses,
exactly what we wore
first day of first grade.
Could have been the two of us
but wasn't.
We didn't meet until
college. . .day one.
Discovered one another at lunch,
discovered we had every class together,
discovered we had so much in common,
discovered we wanted to be roommates,
to always stay in touch.
Forty-eight years, seven grandchildren later
she's still an important part of my life,
now from a great geographical distance. . .
but never far from my heart.

Love one another deeply from the heart. 1 Peter 1:22b NIV

Sweet Selfishness

Trust in the Lord with all your heart, and do not lean on your own under-standing. In all your ways acknowledge him, and he will make straight your paths. Proverbs 3:5-6 ESV

"Beware of the three B's!" we warned our kids before they left for college. Have you heard of the three B's? Chances are, your parents already warned you about them.

Booze, Bills, and Babes. The three dream killers. You've heard the lectures about booze and bills. In a nutshell, don't drink, and live within your means, but what about those babes?

Your parents taught you to get along with others, to share, to be helpful, kind, and unselfish. Now you're living away from home, working toward your goals. You may not know what your ultimate destination will look like, but you are moving in a forward direction toward success. You live among friends and perhaps you've even met someone special, a "babe," someone you hope you can build a future with. You generously and unselfishly give them your time and attention.

May I suggest that there is a sweet sort of selfishness that is pleasing to God?

Stay focused on the plan that's been set before you, even if you aren't yet sure of the final destination. Distractions will come. Friends and "babes" will try to redirect you. They'll entice you with loving promises or dreams they've planned for themselves, won't you join them? Too often, we decide that God must have sent these people to direct us away from our path, to a better one. Often, though, it's a detour. A long, bumpy road around a large messy construction zone that leads right back to the original path. Much later, you merge onto the same road again, alone, and a little ragged and dusty.

The college years are a time for sweet selfishness. This type of selfishness focuses on God and you together, and His plan for your life. Maybe God's plan includes another person and a fusion of your dreams. Stay in close fellowship with the Lord so you will have discernment when distraction comes. If you are aligned with God's plan, you will avoid unnecessary detours!

A Friend Indeed

Some friends don't help, but a true friend is closer than your own family.
Proverbs 18:24 CEV

Looking back on my college days, I was so naive and innocent. Here I was almost 18 yrs old, from a town with one stoplight, headed off to the cement city with traffic jams, diversity of cultures, and millions of people pushing past me.

If it wasn't for my good friend and roommate, I am not sure I would have survived as well as I did. We were together for car trouble in the inner city, late night studying and preparing for projects, and talks and tears because of heartbreak and what socials to attend. We lived on canned peas, macaroni and cheese, and spam...and we survived!

A true friend is a gift from God. I have no doubt in my mind. We tried to solve the world's problems, helped each other in our faith, learned to roller skate, and raced to class together. The Bible shares several examples of friendship. David had Jonathan, Ruth had Naomi, Elisha had Elijah, and Paul had Silas.

Paul knew what it was to have true blue friends to be there for us but also to help us in our faith journey. In 2 Thessalonians 1:3 (CEV) he says, "My dear friends, we always have good reason to thank God for you, because your faith in God and your love for each other keep growing all the time."

During college life, it is so important to have good, supportive friends that can help this school year. When there are doubts, stress, or times to chill, it is those friends that help us move ahead.

Do you have this kind of friend in your circle this year? Do you and your friends encourage each other in your faith and walk with God?

Loneliness

The eyes of the Lord are on the righteous, and His ears are attentive to their cry. Psalm 34:15 NIV

God is everywhere. That is one of His attributes. I attended college a number of years ago when cell phones or emails were not yet on the scene – I didn't even have a computer (that was a few years later). I remember getting letters or "care packages" from home. I made occasional phone calls and family did the same. I was a part of a Christian group on a secular campus. If you know Jesus Christ as your Savior then you are promised His Presence through the Holy Spirit that dwells within you (John 14-15). What better Friend to have when you're lonely!

Perhaps an email, letter or phone call is needed to a family member or friend when facing loneliness, but remember from the verse above the Lord is watching you and He's also listening to your prayers. Psalm 34:17 reads, "The righteous cry out, and the Lord hears them; he delivers them from all their troubles." Take time to pray to Jesus who is one Friend who will never leave you!

Prayer: Lord Jesus, You know I feel lonely right now. Please, as I read your Word and pray, may I remember that I'm not alone when Your Holy Spirit resides within.

There is No Such Thing
as Leftover Bacon

There is no such thing as leftover bacon. I have never seen it and I am convinced it does not exist. In researching the topic, I have discussed the issue with several people. They have all agreed. Leftover bacon is a myth.

At first, this theory may appear to defy logic. Every other food is capable of producing leftovers. At our house, for example, spaghetti is particularly adept at this. English peas and rice are also very leftover prone. We once had three or four dried dates that sat in a small container in the back of the fridge for almost a year before I finally consumed them and put them out of their misery. But never bacon. Bacon is just too good to be left unconsumed. The demand always meets the supply.

When I die, I don't want to be like spaghetti or English peas. I want to be like bacon. One hundred percent shared out. Every crumb given away. Every bit consumed. Nothing held back. No leftovers.

He who finds his life will lose it, and he who loses his life for My sake will find it. Matthew 10:39 NKJV

Love Unbound

They refused to obey and did not remember the miracles you had done for them. Instead, they became stubborn and appointed a leader to take them back to their slavery in Egypt! But you are a God of forgiveness, gracious and merciful, slow to become angry, and rich in unfailing love. You did not abandon them, even when they made an idol shaped like a calf and said, 'This is your god who brought you out of Egypt!' They committed terrible blasphemies. Nehemiah 9:17-18 NLT

There are times I've been confident I wandered too far from God. Made too many sinful mistakes, sure he didn't want me anymore.

One such time was the night I stayed out with my boyfriend. I started home very early, ashamed. I was the quintessential good girl who cut her teeth on a church pew. But I believed some lies and was being secretly rebellious. On the hour drive home that morning I fell asleep. Awaking only because my car was being violently pulled from the highway into the bar ditch. Following my natural reaction I jerked the car back onto the road rolling a few times before coming to rest on the opposite side of the road. Thankfully, God and my seatbelt protected me. I was sore the next day but otherwise unhurt.

During this rebellious time in my life God never left me. He stayed with me waiting patiently in unfailing love. I wish this wasn't a part of my story, but this is one of the beautiful ways God has drawn me into repentance and unending grace through his forgiveness.

The book of Nehemiah is a memoir about Nehemiah and his work rebuilding Jerusalem and purifying the Jewish people. A picture of God's unfailing love for his beloved even as they rebelled against the love he persistently showed for them.

Count on it. Count on Him. God's grace far exceeds anything our hearts or minds can comprehend. Could there be anything better than being loved by God? It's for us, for today.

Lord Jesus, we need your unfailing love. Please forgive us for the sin that separates us from a relationship with you. Thank you for your grace and mercy. Help us to live a life that is pleasing to you and that demonstrates your character, in Jesus' name, Amen.

Storms of Life

Whenever the rainbow appears in the clouds, I will see it and remember the everlasting covenant between God and all living creatures of every kind on the earth. Genesis 9:16 NIV

My husband's grandmother lay dying in the hospital. Weeks before she had broken her wrist. Now, a staff infection raged within her frail body. My husband, who had lived with his grandmother while he attended college a few years earlier, felt heavy with concern.

Although she remained stable enough for us to pay her several hospital visits, her impending death loomed over us. A couple weeks later, my husband's parents called to say his grandmother had passed away.

After receiving this solemn news, I suggested to my husband, "Let's take a drive." Gloomy rain showers poured over our windshield as we traveled to a nearby lake. Suddenly, glancing up, we noticed a vibrant rainbow spread out across the horizon. In minutes, the sky had transformed from a gloomy backdrop to a canvas full of amazing colors.

On our drive home, my husband and I sensed God's Spirit assuring us of His compassionate love. As with Noah, He reminded us He would rebuild and bless our lives. How good to know the Lord remains faithful throughout the storms of our lives.

Prayer: Thank you, God, for displaying your love through nature. We know we can count on your love to comfort us as we experience the inevitable losses that come with life on earth. In Jesus' name. Amen

Too Much Love in the Air

During college I lived with three girlfriends...and their respective boyfriends. Actually, only four of our names were on the lease, but the guys hung out at our place so often they became like honorary roommates. Many evenings when I felt overwhelmed by too much "love in the air," I would take a study break on our apartment's roof. There I watched the stars twinkling above the city skyline. There I wrapped my arms around myself to guard against the wind, as well as comfort the ache in my heart.

It's so hard watching them with their boyfriends, I cried. Why am I the only one who hasn't found someone?

I didn't want to be alone anymore. My sinking self-esteem craved for a guy's attention. I pleaded for God to bring me a boyfriend right now – no, preferably yesterday! But He had something else to address first.

Do you trust Me?

I had fallen to the bottom of a well of self-pity when this question met me like a rope unfurled to my rescue. Did I trust God? Sure, I knew many of the Bible verses about trusting Him. I had even memorized Proverbs 3:5-6 NIV: "Trust in the Lord with all your heart and lean not on your own understanding; in all your ways submit to him, and he will make your paths straight." Yet, did I trust Him enough to submit this part of my life to Him? Did I believe He would bring the right guy into my life at the right time? To be honest, I didn't. The last thing I wanted to do was be patient.

In the following months, however, waiting became an unexpected blessing. Through my times on the rooftop, I became aware of God's constant presence. As I witnessed my roommates' relationships end one by one, I thanked God for protecting me from heartbreak. Moreover, I came to see that while a relationship can provide companionship, it is not a perfect or everlasting solution. Only God's love can fulfill our deepest longings.

If you are struggling with feelings of loneliness, my prayer is that you would look to the Lord. His love for you is complete and drama-free. Trust Him to meet your every need because you are so precious to Him!

Stolen Cheese

*Trust in the Lord with all your heart and lean not on your own under-
standing. In all your ways acknowledge Him and He shall direct your
paths. Proverbs 3:5-6 ESV*

I was nicely into my book when I heard the rustle of a napkin.
Looking up I glimpsed Bogart, my Great Dane, with his nose on my
plate. On closer inspection there was a piece of cheese somewhat hidden
in his clenched jaw. Leaping up I cried in my authoritative voice, "Drop
it!" (He is not allowed people food. It gives him noxious gas.)

Looking guilty, he immediately hit the floor. Unfortunately the
piece of cheese was still firmly buried in his massive jowls. He had not
chewed or swallowed, but I knew it would not be given up easily. In
an instant, a battle ensued.

The higher I stood, the lower he crouched. His eyes rolled in my
direction but his jaw remained firmly clamped. In a flash I was on his
back gripping his jaws, prying one up and the other down.

Slowly an opening appeared and I continued to shake the pre-
mentioned food out of his cavernous mouth. As the spoil of war dropped
to the floor we both lunged for it, ending up sprawled on the ground.
My hands work better than his and I finally came up with the prized
slimy piece of cheese. I arose victor, slightly bruised, and covered in
drool and dog hair, but victor none-the-less.

Such a struggle to hold on to something of little importance...and
it was always the same whether cheese, used tissue, or my hairbrush.
(Yes those are his favorites.)

A consuming amount of effort for no gain-just like my wrestling
matches with God.

Thinking back over my Christian walk, there have been many times
I've held onto things I had no right to. We all have.

Whether an unhealthy relationship or a consuming fear, impure
thoughts or a spirit of unforgiveness, any disobedience we allow a hold
on our hearts will hinder our witness and rob us of peace, limiting the
power of God in our lives. He may have to shake us by our heart muscle
to make us let go. The longer we struggle the messier it gets.

Let's walk in obedience, holding only onto the Word of God and
His promises, and watch His amazing power work through us.

Finding Balance

*Look carefully then how you walk….making the best use of the time,
because the days are evil. Ephesians 5:15,16 ESV*

The prospect of college intimidated me. Afraid I would fail, I determined to work hard—very hard. I spent every evening at the library. Even on Saturdays I got up early to study. My conscientious habits paid off with Highest Honors.

Can a student be too disciplined? Too driven?

What about you? Do you wrestle with guilt when you're not hitting the books? Or does social media nibble away at higher priorities? No matter where you find yourself, locating a healthy balance between academics, relationships, work, rest, and play is a life-long pursuit. Looking back, I should have placed more me-space in my life. I didn't get enough sleep, didn't eat well, and didn't lighten the stress in constructive ways.

I had a friend who often said, "There is always time to do the will of God." Now my husband, he's the guy who picked me up from the library at 9 p.m. He brought a little balance to my life. Still does.

In Solomon's collection of Proverbs, he praises hard work and condemns laziness. In Ecclesiastes 3, he notes the many seasons in life and how God designates specific times for specific activities. He advises his readers to find moderation in their living and even admits that "much study is a weariness of the flesh" (Ecclesiastes 12:12).

Jesus' life modeled balance. With his disciples, He traveled from place to place to teach kingdom truths, healing many along the way. When pressed by the crowds with little time to even eat, Jesus said to them, "Come away by yourselves to a desolate place and rest a while" (Mark 6:31).

Finding balance isn't something we can check off a list. It's a prayerful practice. A daily listening to God's voice. Input from others can help us find perspective, along with the ancient writings of a wise king named Solomon.

Redeem the time and pursue balance. Do the will of God.

Lion in Wait

*Be sober, be vigilant; because your adversary the devil walks about like a
roaring lion, seeking whom he may devour. 1 Peter 5:8 NKJV*

From the friends we allow to speak into our lives to the books we
read or the movies we watch, we, as Christians, are to remain aware
and alert of the world around us. I learned this lesson the hard way
by becoming distracted by the "things" around me. The devil (Satan)
used the opportunity to lead me down a road of poor choices (drinking,
partying, inappropriate relationships, etc.) none of which brought honor
or glory to God.

What's so important about remaining vigilant anyway? Peter gives
us the answer in 1 Peter 5:8, Satan is looking for us to be caught off
guard so he can pounce on us like prey and then devour us. Yikes! I
know I'm caught off guard when I take my focus off Christ and put it
on the "stuff" of my day.

Curious, I Googled "how do lions hunt." According to natural-
highsafaris.com, "…lions stalk from cover to cover with a final burst
of speed at the end or they find a bush close to something the prey
needs – usually water – climbs in and waits."

Lions are incredibly good at hiding and remarkably patient. The
Bible says Satan roams throughout the earth (Job 1:7) like a roaring
lion looking for whom he may devour (1 Peter 5:8). He hides in things
that are good and then waits for us to take them to the extreme.

While in college, I spent my time going to dinner with friends,
participating in theatre events, playing collegiate sports, and taking
weekend drives to the mountains. There is nothing wrong with any of
these things. What I didn't realize is Satan was "lurking" in them ready
to pounce. I made choices that lead me away from my quiet time and
prayer. With my eyes clearly off of Christ, Satan planted seeds of doubt
and fear tearing down any sense of confidence and security.

To remain vigilant:
- Start your day with Bible reading and prayer. Then listen.
- Practice Christ's presence by talking to Him throughout the day.
- Surround yourself with friends who will hold you accountable.

There may be bumps along the way, but with your focus firmly on
Christ, Satan will have to find someone else to devour.

No Strings Attached

In this you greatly rejoice, though now for a little while, if need be, you have been grieved by various trials, that the genuineness of your faith, being much more precious than gold that perishes, though it is tested by fire, may be found to praise, honor, and glory at the revelation of Jesus Christ, whom having not seen you love. 1 Peter 1:6-8a NKJV

Clouds drift, some slower than others, depending on the wind speed. Though they seem to be following us, it is us keeping up with the clouds. If we will stop for just a moment, and allow time for the clouds to pass by, we will once again feel that warmth of the sun that never stopped shining, and the darkness soon disappears.

I sometimes endure a cloud of despair that looms over my head. This cloud or what I deem as a bad-circumstance at times seems unshakable. Then I pause and remind myself…This cloud is not a kite – there are no strings attached!

Every event in our life comes before the Son of God, Jesus – just as it did in the Bible, in the Book of Job. The Lord sees, hears, feels, and knows everything we go through. These trials and life's events don't take Him by surprise, and He will use them to refine our faith.

If you are experiencing your own cloud of despair with no end in sight; and it seems like the sun in your life will not shine again, I encourage you to allow the gentle breeze of the Holy Spirit to blow that cloud away. Don't hold on to it, cut the string – and let it go! Allow the Son of God to shine and then bask in His everlasting peace. This trial you are enduring is but for a season – and it too shall pass.

Perfume

What cologne do you dab on before heading out the door for your classes?

My favorite perfume is distilled from lemon verbena grown in the south of France. I once visited a museum there full of antique copper stills and clear glass flasks and wooden vats retaining the breath of essence left over from long-ago steeping of blossoms collected in the surrounding fields—rose, lavender, mimosa, and jasmine.

God uses the sense of smell in His Word to illustrate His nature and our proper response.

We read that, in Bible times, camel caravans bore aromatic cargo of herbs, spices, fruits, and flowers throughout the Ancient Near East for barter and peace offering. Esteemed guests, sprinkled with fragrant waters of friendship, were served banquets seasoned with anise, cumin, cinnamon, fennel, and saffron. Linens were perfumed. Wounds were cleansed and infections treated with pungent balm of Gilead, a salve symbolizing spiritual healing as well.

Worship of a holy God came to involve the olfactory system. Noah disembarked from the ark to offer burnt sacrifice, its pleasing odor rising to the heavens. Jacob awoke from his ladder dream to anoint his stone pillow with infused oil in gratitude for God's grace. Incense used during Tabernacle worship set apart people for God's special use, as Israel was declared a sweet savor brought out from among the nations. For generations, scented smoke hovered above the Ark of the Covenant, billowing out from the Holy of Holies to announce God's glorious presence in Spirit.

And then God came in the flesh; Jesus was born to gifts of myrrh and frankincense befitting royalty. Near the end of His life, Mary bathed His feet with costly nard, the ambrosia filling the room to picture the sacrifice He was about to make upon the Cross. The final book of the Bible describes golden bowls full of incense—the prayers of the saints.

Thus, biblical smells symbolize peace, hospitality, and healing by a holy, gracious God whom we worship through our practices and our prayers because He sent salvation in Jesus as a "fragrant offering and sacrifice" on our behalf.

When you spritz on your eau de toilette today, remember that you yourself emanate a certain bouquet as you lovingly spread the knowledge of God in telling others the gospel story. You are the "aroma of Christ" to God and the "fragrance of life" to those in your classroom.

But thanks be to God, who . . . through us spreads the fragrance of the knowledge of him everywhere. For we are the aroma of Christ to God . . . a fragrance from life to life. 2 Corinthians 2:14-16 ESV

Walk in love, as Christ loved us and gave himself up for us, a fragrant offering and sacrifice to God. Ephesians 5:2 ESV

No Coincidence

*Surely God is my salvation; I will trust and not be afraid. The Lord, the
Lord himself, is my strength and my defense. He has become my salvation.*
Isaiah 12:2 NIV

Our daughter, Lisa, went off to college feeling fearful and lonely.
But knowing where to turn, she asked God to find her a new home
church where she could receive the love and support she needed. A
small church in her new community advertised on campus its desire
to serve the Lord through a campus ministry. Lisa went there, entered
the program, and was paired with the Browns, a family with four small
children. They welcomed and embraced her as family and asked her to
live with them during her sophomore year.

When my husband, my mother-in-law, and I went to their home to
meet them, they greeted us warmly and told us that Lisa had become
like family to them. At that moment we didn't realize how true that
statement was. Mom walked over to their living room mantel, pointed
to a picture of an older woman and exclaimed, "That's my cousin!"
Mr. Brown replied, "That's my mother!" Again Jesus made a way and
brought Lisa to exactly the right place at the right time.

No matter what our situation, when we take our needs to Jesus,
He meets them in His time.

Love Wrapped Up in a Hamburger

Taste and see that the Lord is good; blessed is the man who takes refuge in him. Psalm 34:8 NIV

I had to restrain myself from gulping the hamburger down in one bite; the tantalizing grill smell was that inviting. The wrapper almost unfolded by itself. For a poor college student, a grand feast awaited.

As I entered college, I was blessed in many ways—scholarships, loans, and (later) part-time jobs. But I was also poor. Cash-poor. And it was at night, after the cafeteria closed and my meal ticket remained useless until breakfast the next morning, when I always seemed to be the hungriest. Of course there was always the snack bar after hours, but that necessitated...money.

Oh, how I guarded any loose change I could gather. For I knew that a trip to the snack bar would come only if I saved up for it. And then, when I did collect the amount I needed and knew I could afford my tasty treat, I headed out. The night sky might be clear with stars shining. The air might be chilly, and I'd have to zip my jacket collar to my neck. But always, believe it or not, I slowed my steps in anticipation of what was coming. Finally I placed my order, paid my bill, and waited. When ready, I carried my treasure to a table and unwrapped it slowly, and, bite-by-savoring-bite, I enjoyed. To this day the memory is still pleasant.

The hamburger was a gift. Wrapped in all the trimmings it represented God's message to me: "I love you. You are my child, and I care about you. Along the way, no matter the struggles that might come, I will give you reminders of my love. Just come to me and unwrap. Taste of my goodness. I am here for you."

At God's table, love rules—no matter what's on the menu.

God's Purpose in You

I know that You can do everything, And that no purpose of Yours can be withheld from You. Job 42:2 NKJV

God sometimes uses loss and suffering for His glorious purpose in our lives. Job's suffering was not without purpose. It revealed the character of God to Job, showing a God who is deeply aware of our problems, and a God who goes before us and who stands with us as we endure. But Job's suffering also revealed the character of God in Job. In this same way our suffering is not without purpose in our lives. How we handle suffering will demonstrate the character of God in us.

After having questioned God's purpose in allowing loss and pain in His life, Job does not cry out for justice, but instead confesses to God that He has spoken about things he knows nothing about. What an amazing confession followed by his proclamation in Job 42:2. Job has realized he is nothing in the presence of a holy God. Earlier Job had maintained his righteousness and integrity. But having seen the Lord, all he can now say is, "I repent in dust and ashes" (42:6).

Even though Job had questions, even though Job wrestled with doubt, once the Lord reminded Job of His purpose for all of creation, Job acknowledged that God can achieve all that He plans, and that His plan is sovereign because He can do all things (Matthew 19:26). He is the author and finisher of our faith (Hebrews 12:2) and He knows the beginning from the end (Isaiah 46:10). He is a jealous God and desires complete surrender of our will to His purposes (Deuteronomy 6:15), but He is also a God of tender mercies (Lamentations 3:22-23).

We may have questions. We may not know the answers. We may not understand why the Lord gives and takes away, but we, like Job, can proclaim, "I know that you can do everything, and that no purpose of Yours can be withheld from You."

God is a God of purpose, and there is no circumstance in our lives that is without His purpose to complete the work He began in each of us (Philippians 1:6). Like Job, sometimes it is only our perspective that hinders God's work from being done.

Meditation: Are you so caught up in your own pain and suffering that you miss seeing the purpose in God's amazing plan for your life?

Healthy Choices

I am the bread of life. John 6:35a HCSB

Do you love the smell of fresh baked bread? I love making home-made bread. Especially whole wheat bread made from freshly milled flour. Did you know that bread made from freshly milled whole wheat flour has 40 of the 44 known vitamins and minerals that our body needs for good health? It is no wonder that Jesus continually referred to himself as the "Bread of Life." It is amazing how much better we feel when we are eating foods that are good for us and give us the nutrition that our body needs to work as God created.

Does God really care about our physical health just as He does our spiritual health? 1 Corinthians 10:31 HCSB tells us, "Therefore, whether you eat or drink, or whatever you do, do everything for God's glory." So in other words, yes. Did you know there are over 600 dietary references found in scripture? God tells us to let everything that we do glorify Him, including what we put into our bodies. When we are physically unhealthy, it robs us of the energy to be able to do the things that God has called us to do.

Most all college students have heard about the Freshman 15. It refers to the weight gain that most college freshmen tend to gain during the first year of college due to late-night eating, all-you-can-eat dining halls, and lack of substantial exercise. It is easy to eat on the run between classes and late at night while studying. Generally, those food choices tend to be unhealthy choices with lots of fat and calories. Just as Christ wants us to be spiritually healthy, He also wants us to be physically healthy. Making good food choices help us have the energy and vitality needed to make it through the busy and hectic days of a college student. How we treat our bodies now will also affect our quality of life later on. If we want to live a long, productive life, then it starts now by making healthy choices.

Dear Lord, help me glorify You in everything I do. Today, give me the strength to make good food choices. Help me eat things that are good for me and that will keep me physically healthy today and in the years to come. Amen.

Beauty From Ashes

I was fast approaching my 15th birthday when devastating news reached me: The school I had attended from first grade had burned the night before. Nothing was left but the charred walls.

When I heard the heartbreaking news, I cried. I was afraid I would be sent to a different school than my classmates because I lived in another town and rode a bus to school. I was a shy teen and the thought of being forced to attend school with strangers filled me with fear.

Imagine my joy when I learned only a day before my birthday that all of my high school would be combined with another small school eleven miles from my home. I would eventually graduate with my classmates.

Those first days in my new school were filled with anxious anticipation as I wondered how we would be accepted by the other students. Would they resent our coming and causing confusion and crowding in their school?

My worries were needless because the students and teachers not only accepted us, they went out of their way to help us to adjust to the new surroundings.

Isaiah 61:3 (NIV) gives this promise: "...to bestow on them a crown of beauty instead of ashes, the oil of gladness instead of mourning and a garment of praise, instead of a spirit of despair." Out of the ashes of sorrow and anxiety grew a beauty of unity of helpfulness and encouragement between our two schools.

Now when I think about that stressful time, I am reminded that God has been faithful in my past and he will be faithful in my present and in my future. He will work in and through whatever heartache, sorrow, or pain I encounter.

God continues to work to bring beauty from the ashes of my life. He will do the same for you if you allow Him to guide your life.

Out of Bounds

Keeping healthy boundaries is an important challenge in a world that is filled with intruders.

Everyone else seems to have "big plans for your life" and insist on bombarding you with them. Sales people on radio, television, newspaper, cell phones, and even social media are all lined up for your ear.

The wisest advisor in our life is so often neglected – the Word of God. The Bible has much to say about maintaining healthy relationships.

Here are some tips I like to think about as my *Nuggets of Gold*:

- A forgiving attitude allows us to be emotionally free toward those who hurt us. Matthew 6:14
- A cooperative attitude toward others opens your heart to receive, Proverbs 2:1-5
- A loving attitude lets us be free from selfish frustration. I Corinthians 13
- An understanding attitude allows us to see God's eternal purpose in all that happens. Romans 8:28
- A trusting attitude permits us to benefit from others wise counsel. Proverbs 28:26

The longest chapter in the Bible shares this in Psalms 119:2— "Happy are they that keep His testimonies and seek Him with their whole heart."

Keep the Bible close within your boundaries and you are sure to win the game of life.

Time to Change

The whole Bible was given to us by inspiration by God and is useful to teach us what is true and to make us realize what is wrong in our lives; it straightens us out and helps us do what is right. 2 Timothy 3:16 LB

As a young girl, I overheard my aunt warning my mother, "Don't let her go to college. It will change her." Thankfully my parents didn't stand in my way when I earned a scholarship and left home. The potential for change was both exhilarating and disquieting.

I went to college so shy that talking to new people was nearly impossible. I graduated from college with the ability to interact with classmates, teachers, and the public.

I began college with an aptitude for reading, writing, research, and math. I graduated competent to translate research into action, write clear narratives, and use math to solve work problems.

In some ways I had changed.

But, in other ways I had not changed. I left for college with the belief that people should not drink alcohol before the age of 21. There was frequent opportunity to change my belief or behavior, but I chose to refrain from attending the parties where alcohol would be flowing freely. Did I spend some lonely evenings in my dorm room? Yes – until I found like-minded friends!

As author John Maxwell says, "Change is inevitable. Growth is optional."

As young adults, our first years living away from our parents are when we earnestly begin to question many things. It is a normal phase in our development as we define who we are, what we believe, and how we behave. We question the values that our parents instilled in us. We question the beliefs that we have been taught. We question what we learn in class, what we read, and what we view. We even question the wisdom of our own choices.

It is comforting to know that God has said He will never leave us or forsake us (Hebrews 13:5) and nothing can separate us from His love (Romans 8:38-39) – even when we have questions.

He is faithful and true to His Word. We can read what God has to say in the Bible, while praying for God to give us wisdom as we make important life choices about when to change and when to stay the same.

Wonderfully Made

I praise you for I am fearfully and wonderfully made, Marvelous are your works; my soul knows it very well. Psalm 139:14 ESV

"You are fat." "Your skin is pimply." "Why are you so stupid?" These words hurt and are laminated onto our brains at a young age by our society. But they aren't what God thinks of you.

Before I was saved, I believed the words of the enemy and the world. I thought that I needed this product and that product to make me more beautiful. As a teenager, I would leaf through the fashion magazines wishing that I looked how the models looked. At the time, I didn't realize how wrong this thinking was. Even now as a Christian, I still can struggle with self-worth.

Often times we allow this world's values to define who we are. As a Christian, we have identity in Christ and He knew us before we were placed in the womb. God doesn't think that you are ugly, or not smart because He loves you. Most important of all He didn't make you that way. You are a work of art. A masterpiece. An original. Believe that you are perfect just how you are. Embrace this verse in Psalms and don't believe the voice of the enemy.

Let us pray:

Dear heavenly Father,

Help us to trust the verse in Psalms 139:14, that we are beautifully and wonderfully made and not believe the voice of the enemy. Please help us to see ourselves, how you do, and not by what the world considers beauty. In Jesus' name. Amen.

Assured Success

Commit to the Lord whatever you do, and your plans will succeed.
Proverbs 16:3 NIV

The Woman's Club president's husband received an unexpected transfer, leaving me, the vice president, in charge for the next year and a half. I had only accepted this role because it seemed so safe; now I faced an assignment that really took me out of my comfort zone. In fact, it was even daunting.

Needless to say, I offered up many prayers during that time. What was truly amazing, though, was the transformation in my life. Instead of a shy, retiring person I blossomed with leadership skills that truly amazed me and that have been useful throughout the many following years.

The above scripture is a wonderful mantra for anyone's life. Who among us isn't faced with situations that challenge our inmost being? This is especially true of college students—exams, interviews, projects and relationships, to name a few. Just as cell phones today keep us connected horizontally for any emergency, so too a vertical call through prayer to our Heavenly Father will bring the aid we seek. This Bible verse actually carries a promise. It doesn't say our plans could succeed or might succeed. It says that our plans will succeed. What could be better than that!

Belle of the Ball

A young lady was led in to a magnificently decorated ballroom. The man in the distinguished attire made a formal announcement to the guests, as the young lady stood poised in her finest ball gown. Her father was admiring her grace, her beauty and elegance. After the introduction was complete, she made her way through the crowded room. I imagined what it would be like to be introduced as a child of God...

Introducing
A child
Of the King
Branch of the Vine
Joint heir with Christ
Born again of the Spirit
Of the household of God
Of the sheepfold of Christ
Child of the Most High God
A Member of the body of Christ
Crown of righteousness recipient
God's workmanship created in Christ Jesus
Was once dead in sin, but is now made alive
Washed and sanctified by the blood of the Lamb who
Takes away the sins of the world
Amen!

Then I thought how I would not need an introduction to God's kingdom, because I am His and He is mine and I belong to God through Christ. He has known me since before I was born. He is all-knowing and omniscient. He is seated in the heavenly places. He is the mighty King of Kings and Lord of Lords!

Matthew 18:3; John 15:5; Romans 8:17; John 3:3; Ephesians 2:19; 2 Samuel 7:8; Romans 8:16; Romans 12:5; 2 Timothy 4:8; Ephesians 2:10; Ephesians 2:1; 1 Corinthians 6:11; John 1:29; John 17:20-23; Psalm 139:13-14; Psalm 139:1-3; Ephesians 1:20; Revelation 19:16 (Scriptures taken from KJV, NKJV & NIV)

Bible Media

Look carefully then how you walk, not as unwise but as wise, making the best use of the time, because the days are evil. Ephesians 5:15-16 ESV

Like many people these days, my smart phone goes everywhere with me. School, work, grocery, even the bathroom; it's there. I can't even leave it in another room in the house without feeling like I might miss a call or a text. The thought of turning it off for an hour is almost painful. I can't imagine forgetting it when leaving the house… I'd probably turn around and come back for it.

What if I put God's word on the same pedestal that I do my iPhone? What if whenever I had a free minute, I began thumbing through it, not wanting to miss one word or one thought, one parable or one command? What if the God of the universe is trying to get my attention, trying to impart some wisdom or warn me of danger? I shouldn't want to miss that, and yet I do.

I have a free Bible app on my phone. Perhaps instead of Facebook, I will read the book of John, meditating on the precious words that are found there, or maybe I will park in Psalms and enjoy the comfort and challenges found there. Just as there is no end to the information to be found on social media, no end to the different ways to browse and explore, the Bible is rich in information and wisdom. The beauty of it is that the application of the Bible to my life yields godliness and holiness, not just information that may or may not improve my life and is most likely a time waster.

My goal is not to eliminate my social media exposure, but to give God's word equal priority so that He can order my days according to His will. We live in an instant society and everything around us works against quiet, reflective time getting to know the heart and will of our Savior. It's worth the effort to make time, and take advantage of that Bible app, too, so our time on this earth is being directed by and brings glory to God.

Lighthouses

Your word is a lamp for my feet and a light on my path.
Psalm 119:105 HCSB

Lighthouses have been used for centuries to warn sailors to straighten their position so they don't hit land. They are built on islands or beaches and act as guideposts for ships during storms or when it is dark. In early times, people set fires at the edge of the water to warn boats of dangerous rocks and shore lines. The Egyptians were the first to build lighthouses used to guide ships. In 283, the Egyptians completed the tallest lighthouse ever built. It guided ships for over 1,500 years and stood 900 feet tall.

Just as lighthouses are used to guide ships safely to shore and keep them from harm, God's word guides us and helps keep us in the right direction. Going through life without spending time in God's word is like trying to put together a puzzle without a picture to help you know how the pieces fit together. It is very important that we make it a priority to spend time in God's word every day. James 4:8 tells us to "draw near to God, and He will draw near to you." College life is full of many choices and decisions. Meditating daily on God's word can help us make choices and decisions that are pleasing to God and are in alignment with His Word. But college life can get very hectic. It is very easy to let other things take priority over spending time in God's word. Studying for tests, writing papers, and having fun with friends seem to take up most of our time and it is easy to let those things take priority over our time with God. Before we know it, it has been several days or even weeks since we have spent time in God's word. A good practice is to set aside a specific time every day to read God's Word.

Lord, please speak to me today as I read Your Word. Open up my eyes and my heart and help me understand your ways. Lead me in the right direction so that my life glorifies You in everything I do. Help me make choices and decisions that align with Your Word. Amen.

Hidden Temptations

Words of Wisdom: God's provision does not involve immorality.

I learned this the hard way. There was this whole ordeal in college with a project I didn't have time to finish, a ruined template on which the previous user saved his finished project and my stupidity in thinking God provided this opportunity as a blessing for me. When in reality, it was called cheating! Thankfully, I had an understanding professor who gave me a second chance.

Has this ever happened to you? Have you ever mistaken a moment of temptation as a provision from God?

This reminds me of the adage, "If it seems to good to be true, it probably is." God does provide in miraculous ways; however, if the provided opportunity is outside the Character of God, then walk away.

Temptations are often camouflaged amid needs.

There are three "keys" to detecting true provision from temptation.

The First Key is learn the character of God. Had I considered God's character prior to my college "incident," it would have been clear to me that a righteous and just God would not provide for me by means claiming someone else's work as my own.

The Second Key is know His Word. The Bible is full of examples and wise words to help. I could have pulled from King David's immoral blunder with Bathsheba or recalled the wisdom from 1 Thessalonians 5:22 which says to refrain from even the appearance of evil.

The Third Key is claim His promises. God promised to supply our needs when we need them (Philippians 4:19), not to give us more than we can handle (1 Corinthians 10:13) and not to abandon us (Hebrews 13:5).

Whatever you are going through today, whatever the temptation, remember who God is. Spend time with Him and know what He says. Then, live in confidence that you have the power of the One True God on your side and He loves you beyond compare.

What, then, shall we say in response to these things? If God is for us, who can be against us? He who did not spare his own Son, but gave him up for us all—how will he not also, along with him, graciously give us all things?
Romans 8:31-32 NIV

Roommate Drama

Get rid of all bitterness, rage and anger, brawling and slander, along with every form of malice. Be kind and compassionate to one another, forgiving each other, just as in Christ God forgave you. Ephesians 4:31-32 NIV

Two pleasant, considerate roommates my first year. Both abandoned college to return to their boyfriends.

The second year, I chose Faye because of all we had in common. From the same state, same major, same... hard to remember now exactly why I thought she was a good fit.

We'd had our little disagreements, but we'd managed to tolerate each other until second semester.

For Christmas, I received an electric popcorn popper. Before the days of microwaves and refrigerators in dorm rooms our only options were hot plates and popcorn poppers. I had seen the disgusting poppers that some girls used—black, greasy streams down the sides from never being washed. I told Faye I wanted mine washed well each time so it wouldn't get gross.

But one afternoon I returned to our room to find an oily popper sitting out. I asked her to wash it. She did, mumbling something about meaning to do it later.

A couple of weeks later, same scenario.

The third time, I lost it. I was furious. I'd just gotten in from dinner, so I simply locked the door. Faye returned without her key because we never locked our dorm rooms. I didn't let her in. I told her firmly why she was locked out and she apologized. Our friends came to plead on her behalf. I was heartless. She could not get in our room—for four hours. She was a conscientious student and was hysterical about work she needed to do for the next day's class. Finally, at bedtime, I opened the door and she stomped in. We hardly spoke for days.

She quit using my popcorn popper; finally we were friends again. She was in my wedding; I was in hers.

But how foolish I was! Why did I put a thing over a relationship? So I didn't like what she did. My reaction was worse than her misdeed. We were supposed to be Christians at a Christian college, for Pete's sake. But neither of us acted Christ-like.

As kids we would wail, "It's not fair!" Our parents tell us all the time that life isn't fair. As Christians, we just have to take the unfairness in stride and show that we're different. We aren't to be jealous, or selfish, or greedy, or dishonest. We simply try to follow Christ and show others his compassion.

Only for God

…go into your room, close the door… Matthew 6:6 NIV

Privately, secretly,
unknown by anyone
except God-
prayer and fasting and giving…
If no one can see
anything differing me
from everyone else
how does witness take place?
Like asking in prayer
that the Holy Spirit
take prayer from me
for one for whom no one prays…
These secret ways of worship
are to praise and honor
our God Who knows all –
and leave the outcomes to Him.

Need Super-Hero Power?

*For I know the plans I have for you, declares the Lord, plans to prosper you
and not to harm you, plans to give you hope and a future.*
Jeremiah 29:11 NIV

It was my last Public Speaking class of the semester and the assignment was a graded impromptu. Students were asked to list three potential topics for their impromptu speech on a sheet of paper. After turning in their folded lists, they had to pick a paper and chose their speech topic from one of the three listed. They had ten minutes to prepare.

One of my students was in a wheel chair. He also had limited control over his arms and hands, so I helped by writing down the thoughts that came to him. As it turned out, only one of the potential topics suited—what power would you choose if you were a super-hero? His first thought, of course, was that he would be able to walk. But as he began to construct his speech he realized the enormity of the task. He had so trained his mind to accept the fact that he would never walk, that he struggled to come up with the benefits! In the end, he told the class that he really didn't need to have a super-hero power at all. He had God. And that was all the power he would ever need.

It was one of those gut-wrenching moments that occurs when you come face-to-face with true courage. Here was a young college student who had learned to accept his limitations and work within them. In the course of the semester, I never saw a trace of self-pity. In fact, he occasionally made jokes about his chair. He knew—really knew—that it could not keep the purposes of God from being fulfilled in his life.

And so it is with each of us. We all have limitations in one form or another. Sometimes God removes them. We experience a miraculous healing, either physical or emotional. Money to pay those college bills appears "out of the blue." But when our constraints are not taken away, I pray we would have a mindset like my friend, Kyle. I pray that we, too, would know that nothing can keep God from completing his plan in us and through us.

The Truth Within

*I am writing these things to warn you about those who want to lead you
astray. But you have received the Holy Spirit, and he lives within you, so
you don't need anyone to teach you what is true. For the Spirit teaches you
everything you need to know, and what he teaches is true—it is not a lie.
So just as he has taught you, remain in fellowship with Christ.*
1 John 2:26-27 NLT

Jud headed for the bathroom and a nice hot shower. He got the
water adjusted to just the right temperature and, stepping in, realized
he'd forgotten his shampoo. He glanced around the room and spotted a
travel size shampoo bottle. Perfect! He grabbed the bottle and proceeded
with his usual hair washing ritual. After his shower back in the living
room Jud admitted borrowing the shampoo and asked his roommate
what kind of shampoo it was because his hair felt oddly greasy. His
roommate busted out laughing, "That's not shampoo, man, that's lotion!"
This case of shampoo fraud was not purposeful and was preventable if
only Jud had known what was inside the bottle.

Deception can be easy to slip into, innocent even. You find yourself
in a situation and before long something just doesn't seem right. As
believers of Christ it is imperative that we guard our faith so that the
truth we have received, as taught by the Holy Spirit and the Bible, guides
us daily. A few practical ways to live a life of faith:

- Only get involved in things that build up your faith.
- Do an honest evaluation of what you believe.
- Ask, "Am I willing to yield myself more and more to what God
wants me to do?"
- Heed to what you believe.

By remaining in fellowship with Jesus you will become more adept
at recognizing truth, which will influence your decisions, helping in
avoiding the pitfalls of sin.

Lord Jesus, thank you for your gifts of the Holy Spirit and the
Word. Guard our hearts and the things you have taught us so that we
can recognize those things that are not of you. In Jesus' name, Amen.

Upset Over Nothing

The Master said, "Martha, dear Martha, you're fussing far too much and getting yourself worked up over nothing. Luke 10:38-41 Message

The past few weeks have been difficult ones for our charity in Haiti. Problems loom as donations have dwindled. I find myself anxious over staff issues and the future of our Mission. The stress presses in on all sides.

My Bible reading today covered the story in Luke when Jesus stopped in for dinner with Martha and Mary. This story has always intrigued me because I sort of take Martha's side in the whole episode. I felt for her when Jesus seemed to poo-poo her stress, sticking up for Mary, who was dodging her responsibilities.

Poor Martha, without warning the Master had just walked through her door and plopped down on her couch weary, worn, and hungry.

I understand the pressures of entertaining in my world, prolific in gadgets to make life easier, but I can't imagine the immediate task Martha was faced with. Preparing dinner back then took a little more work than throwing a pizza in the microwave. She actually had to start with killing the lamb and baking the bread. No easy task.

But as I read that passage again in The Message today, something popped off the page and leapt into my awareness.

Verse 41 says, "Martha, Martha, you are fussing too much and getting upset over nothing. One thing only is essential, and Mary has chosen it."

The words Martha, Martha disappeared and my name took their place. It became, "Heather, Heather, you are fussing too much and getting upset over nothing. One thing only is essential and Mary has chosen it."

The message was clear, I was letting pressures get in the way of 'it' and God wanted that to change, but, what was 'it'?

Softly, God whispered these thoughts.

It is choosing to block out the pressures around me to spend time in His presence.

It is simply sitting at His feet, bringing all my issues to Him in prayer.

It is putting all else aside to soak up His Word until it fills me with peace and assurance of God's promises to help carry my load, whatever that is.

Do you feel the need to put your name in Martha's place and follow Mary's example of resting at Jesus' feet? The Master wants to carry your burden and lighten your load.

Go ahead. You can do...it!

He Knows What You Need

In the same way the Spirit also helps our weakness; for we do not know how
to pray as we should, but the Spirit Himself intercedes for us with groanings
too deep for words; and He who searches the hearts knows what the mind
of the Spirit is, because He intercedes for the saints according to the will of
God. Romans 8:26-27 NASB

I was celebrating my birthday and the only present I wanted was to be able to go home and see my parents. It was a cold January day during my second year of college; a day when I had to drag myself around and choose to do what I knew was expected of me. After classes that day, I supervised a cleaning crew on campus. I finished scrubbing the toilets and put the supplies away. On my way back to check on the rest of the crew, I stopped at a window and stared out at the bleak, snowy landscape of the Prairies. The sidewalk was empty except for one lone figure I spotted in the distance. Something about the person's gait was very familiar. As the individual came closer, I felt a lump growing in my throat. I raced down the stairs, out the door and into the open arms of my father. He surprised me with a visit for my birthday.

Many parents delight in doing special things for their children, whether it's meeting physical needs or surprising them with special gifts. God, as our heavenly Father, also delights in granting what we need. The Bible tells us He is able to do much more than we ask or think (Ephesians 3:20-21).

I don't know what your needs are today, but God does. He loves you with His perfect love. He has good plans for you (Jeremiah 29:11). He delights in you more than any doting parent ever could. This doesn't mean that your life will be easy. In fact, Jesus warned us that we would experience "tribulation" or troubles. However, He also promised His peace and strength (John 16:33).

Take a few minutes and tell your heavenly Father what is on your heart today. Bring your requests to him with confidence, knowing that He has the power to do anything. Then trust Him. He knows what you need.

Remarkably and Wonderfully Made

We live in a world that is obsessed with physical beauty. I have been and I am still guilty of constantly sizing myself up to the media's idea of beauty. It is hard not to. We see gorgeous, sculpted bodies, flawless skin and hair. It is easy to become discouraged. Our world has put a high price on being thin and beautiful.

It is a constant spiritual battle to avoid comparing myself to others. It's not just about physical appearance either. In high school, above average grades were easy for me. Studying was rare. While I was at a small college where it wasn't hard to be accepted, some of my former classmates were at MIT, Boston University, even studying overseas and here I was having trouble in what was almost like a big brother to high school. I figured out that I didn't even know how to study. I rarely saw B's and C's and most of the time I was just relieved to get a passing score. It was such a discouraging time. I received my Associate of Sciences degree from that little college.

It was a victory, but for years when asked if I had a degree I would say, "Just an Associates' degree." The Lord began to humble me in His way. He showed me that there are people in the world who never even have the opportunity for a middle school level of education, let alone go to college. I had been so prideful and selfish. The Lord made a way for me to get that education through jobs and financial aid. I began to be proud of where I graduated because I had to claw my way through that degree.

Women and men alike struggle with comparison. The Lord wants us to try our best, but problems come when we let Satan tell us we aren't good enough. As soon as you hear those thoughts you must deny them.

Psalm 139:13-14 HCSB reminds us: For it was You who created my inward parts; You knit me together in my mother's womb. I will praise You, because I have been remarkably and wonderfully made. Your works are wonderful, and I know this very well.

So the next time you doubt yourself, say the above scripture out loud and remind yourself that God is perfect. He does not make mistakes. His works are wonderful, and YOU are one of His works. You are as amazing and beautiful and unique as a sunset. You are remarkable and wonderful.

Teachers are People Too

While driving down a country road, we passed a man jogging. "Hey! That's Mr. Scott – a science teacher from school," my 13 year old daughter, Katie, pointed out. "I can't believe he's exercising like a regular person."

"Aren't teachers regular people?" I asked with a laugh.

"I suppose, but it's hard to think of them that way. I was in second grade before I realized that teachers don't live at school," she explained. "I always thought they just slept in their rooms."

Later, I discovered that all three of my children, including the oldest who is a college student, have trouble imagining their teachers as real people – people who have families, pets, and homes; who shop, do laundry, and cook meals; and who have hobbies and take vacations. It's hard for them to see teachers who make rules, lecture, give assignments, and grade papers as having lives outside of the classroom.

It's part of human nature that we are at least somewhat self-centered. We know the intimate details of our own lives, complete with its joys and difficulties. We know the details of the lives of family and friends who willingly share what they are experiencing and feeling. But it's nearly impossible to comprehend the hardships of others when there's no communication.

When we only understand life from our own viewpoint, it can be hard to feel compassion for others. When Lynn notices that her literature teacher is always in a bad mood, she judges the teacher's behavior from her own point of view. What Lynn doesn't know is that her teacher had a baby over the summer and hasn't had a full night's sleep in months.

The reality is that teachers are real people, with real problems. The absent-minded professor might be going through a divorce. The instructor who reports grades late may be sick from the side effects of chemotherapy. The teacher who doesn't respond to emailed questions might go home each night to care for both an invalid parent and a chronically ill child.

In the same way, teachers only know what students tell them; so students might consider sharing extraordinary circumstances if there is a practical reason to do so.

The Bible gives advice on one way to cope with difficult teachers: pray for them.

I urge, then, first of all, that requests, prayers, intercession and thanksgiving be made for everyone – for kings and all those in authority, that we may live peaceful and quiet lives in all godliness and holiness. This is good, and pleases God our Savior, who wants all men to be saved and to come to a knowledge of the truth. I Timothy 2:1-4 NIV

God's Candy Hearts

It's February and the store shelves are lined with boxes of pastel candy hearts. The pink, lavender, and green confections stamped with sentiments like, "Luv U," "Be Mine," and "Miss You" send sweet little messages.

This morning I read the sentiments while nibbling on a few of the candies and thought opening this little box of candy is like opening my Bible each morning and finding a message from the Lord. Even many of the messages are the same. For example:

Candy Heart	Scripture (New International Version)
Call home	Call to me and I will answer you. Jeremiah 33:3
Chill out	Don't be anxious about anything. Philippians 4:6
Take a Walk	This is the way; walk in it. Isaiah 30:21
Let's Eat	I will come in and eat with him and he with me. Rev. 3:20
I'm Yours	So you will be my people, & I will be your God. Jer. 30:22
Forgiven	Your sins have been forgiven. 1 John 2:12
Everlasting Love	I have loved you with an everlasting love. Jeremiah 31:3

While the candy company prints their messages on sugar, the Lord wants to stamp his message on my heart. And just like I have to nibble on the candy to taste its sweet goodness, I have to spend time in the Word to "taste and see that the Lord is good" (Psalm 34:8). I'm already wondering what message I will find tomorrow.

I Don't Know What to Do

Very early in the morning, while it was still dark, Jesus got up, left the house and went off to a solitary place, where He prayed. Mark 1:35 NIV

I have found myself in this same position, in college and out, where I didn't know what God's will for my life was. I didn't have a clue which direction to take. If I was to advise myself now I would have went away somewhere, even if it was only to the local park, and spend some time in prayer and Bible reading.

The college I attended was located on the shore of Lake Ontario. It would be a great place, that solitary place, to pray and read the Bible. I might have gone to the shore several times during my college days, but it's important to find that solitary place—even if it's a closet in your dorm room. Proverbs 16:9 reads, "In their hearts humans plan their course, but the Lord establishes their steps."

It has now been some time since college days. Looking back I wish now I had prayed more spending much more time in that 'solitary place'. We come to that proverbial fork in the road and wonder which branch to take. Proverbs 1:7 says, "The fear of Lord is the beginning of knowledge, but fools despise wisdom and instruction." Prayer and the reading of God's Word is a necessary avenue to finding God's will for your life. Find that solitary place and find direction for in James 1 it says that God will give wisdom if we only ask!

Prayer: Lord Jesus, I don't know which way to go. Guide me in the direction I should take and give me Your peace. Amen.

Beyond Appearances

But the Lord said to Samuel, "Do not look on his appearance or on the height of his stature, because I have rejected him. For the Lord sees not as man sees: man looks on the outward appearance, but the Lord looks on the heart." 1 Samuel 16:7 ESV

Over the last few years, I have had the privilege of getting to know a remarkable woman, former Paralympian Deborah L. Willows.

Deb has cerebral palsy and has been in a wheelchair for several decades. When she was very young, her parents were encouraged to put her in an institution. Fifty years ago doctors didn't think parents were capable of meeting the needs of their physically challenged sons and daughters.

The Willows would hear nothing of it and proceeded to raise her as they would any child. They always expected their daughter to do her best and become all she could be.

Of course having limited control of her arms and legs, Deb needed assistance. However, that didn't stop her from far exceeding the expectations of many.

One day while watching Olympic swimmers, she said, "I want to do that."

Many parents would have said it was impossible and encouraged her to pursue a more attainable goal, but not the Willows.

Through diligence and determination, Deb set many world records and earned countless medals. Teachers, counselors, and doctors said she would achieve very little. But by God's grace, she proved them wrong.

When you look at others – and yourself – what do you see?

Do you look beyond the external?

Ask God to give you a pure heart and the strength to accomplish all He has planned and purposed for you.

Feeding Time

Jesus answered by quoting Deuteronomy: "It takes more than bread to stay alive. It takes a steady stream of words from God's mouth."
Matthew 4:4 Message

The temptation to hit the snooze button one more time, thus skipping breakfast, dangled in front of me many times my junior year in college. The 18-hour class load, coupled with being an RA and working in the copy room often left me short on sleep. I needed eight hours to feel good, but that was not happening. However, I knew from my mother, a registered nurse, that I needed to eat. Since then, as I taught school for 30+ years, I have seen personally the link between eating properly and being able to study effectively.

If we skip reading God's Word daily, isn't it the same as not eating properly? In this age of smart phones, iPads, etc., it's very easy to have a constant reminder of God's goodness with us at all times. The plethora of daily online devotionals offers something for everyone. My favorite is Jesus Calling by Sarah Young. I also enjoy Turning Point and In Touch, and there are others out there which speak to specific situations.

Let me encourage you to take one scripture daily and devour it. Let it soak into your soul. Put it on your homepage or desktop. Years later, when need arises, God will bring those memorized scriptures to mind. They will become a source of great strength and inspiration as you journey in this troubled world.

Remember this promise:

My God will supply all that you need from His glorious resources in Christ Jesus. Philippians 4:19 Phillips

Adventuring On

It's time to go out into the world
make your mark and claim your stake,
After years of schooling you're now an adult
the world awaits your quake.
It may seem scary at the start
but God will lead the way,
Have faith in Him in all you do
And don't forget to pray.
You're well equipped to begin this adventure
and you can rest assured,
Your education will pay off
along with how you have matured.
God will always be with you
and life's journey will be unclear,
the thrill is exploring your talents
and putting them into high gear.
It's time to discover, you have a new quest
think about Romans twelve,
There is the meaning of adventure,
And that is where you must delve.
So take off with spirit and energy
The world awaits your attendance,
Today is when your adventure begins
the roadway to independence.

So we are to use our different gifts in accordance with the grace that God has given us. If our gift is to speak God's message, we should do it according to the faith that we have; if it is to serve, we should serve; if it is to teach, we should teach; if it is to encourage others, we should do so. Whoever shares with others should do it generously; whoever has authority should work hard; whoever shows kindness to others should do it cheerfully.
Romans 12:5-8 GNT

Money Issues

Do not be anxious about anything, but in everything by prayer and
supplication with thanksgiving let your requests be made known to God.
Philippians 4:6 ESV

My parents served as missionaries in my growing up years. Our family had money for day-to-day expenses, but not much else. When it came time for me to start college, I had eight hundred dollars, which I saved while working two months between my high school graduation and the start of Bible College classes. Common sense told me I should take a year off. However, my parents encouraged me to start college immediately and trust God to provide.

Hudson Taylor said, "God's work done in God's way will never lack God's supply." Paul urged the Philippians not to worry about anything, including their financial needs (vs. 6). Instead, he encouraged them to be thankful and tell God about their needs. Later on in the same chapter, Paul reminds the Philippians that God is able to meet their needs out of the vastness of his riches (vs. 19).

I used the money I had to pay the first installment for Bible College. After Christmas I had to pay the balance. I tried to focus on my studies instead of fretting. One morning we were given information about a financial need bursary. A week or so after I filled out the required paperwork, I was informed that I qualified for one of the bursaries. That was a great encouragement to me. However, when I figured out my expenses for the year, it was apparent I would be short by eight hundred dollars. School continued. One day I received a phone call from a police officer that had been one of my high school teachers. I hadn't heard from him for a couple of years. He informed me God prompted him to phone and find out how college was going for me. I told him about my classes and the things I was learning. Then he asked how I was doing financially. I told him I was short of money. A couple weeks later, I received a check for eight hundred dollars.

I don't know what your needs are, but God does. Be faithful in what He's called you to, and trust Him to meet your needs. Then watch what He does.

Defying the "Dude Paradox"

Do nothing from selfish ambition or conceit, but in humility count others more significant than yourselves. Let each of you look not only to his own interests, but also to the interests of others. Philippians 2:3-4 ESV

Dudes say things like, "Dude, can you set me up with a pro deal?" or "Dude, no friends on a powder day."

A dude's concern for others rarely reaches beyond what someone else can supply him. A dude will listen to your struggles but only to reassure himself his life is better than yours. A dude doesn't come prepared because they assume they can mooch off you.

I remember approaching fellow engineering students in the basement of the library. Not knowing anyone, I approached a study group, "Duuuuude, can I see how you solved the homework?"

The expression dude can be endearing like that of a close confidant. But frequently a dude's true intent is insincere friendship; hijacking what is intended for kindheartedness. In my selfish state, I often use the term dude simply because I don't know their name. My focus is too superficial to connect in a more friendly way.

The truth is, we all have dude expressions. When I endeavor to align my life as a true follower of Jesus, my aspirations turn toward valuing others, as I might honor myself.

The paradox arises from our predisposition toward selfish ambition and vein conceit. To be authentic to obey Jesus' teaching is to set aside our tendency toward self-centeredness.

The Apostle Paul offers a surefire approach to being a good friend in his letter to the people of Philippi.

"In humility." We are to moderate our own pride and confidence in the flesh. The surpassing value of knowing Christ far outweighs our present needs and wants. Like Jesus we are to take on the life of a servant.

"Count others more significant than yourselves." Jesus is our portion, our rock, and our salvation. Declaring our concern for others is a reflection of His sacrifice for us.

"Look not only to his own interests, but also to the interest of others." Unified we become the church. Considering the interests of others builds the church.

Jesus is embodied when you demonstrate the appearance of servant hood to others. We can reclaim the term dude as an appealing sentiment of authentic friendship and scrap the tendency toward insincerity. Yes, it is ostensibly paradoxical.

A Price for Popularity

Don't let anyone look down on you because you are young, but set an example for the believers in speech, in conduct, in love, in faith and in purity. I Timothy 4:12 NIV

When I was in high school, I had a reputation for being "goody-goody." The teachers loved me, but I was jealous of the popular girls.

So I decided to change my actions—to show my classmates that I was not always good—that, in fact, I could be just the opposite. I peppered my language with profanity and was not as pure as I should have been in my relationships with boys. I repeated jokes that I wouldn't have told to my parents or teachers. In trying to fit in, I ruined any good influence I might have had on my classmates.

And I lied to my parents about where I was going and who would be in the car. Finally one night my lies caught up with me and I was so grounded I thought I'd never see the light of day. And of all the things my parents said at the time, something they said later hurt the most. My mother told her best friend, my dear Aunt Beck, about my lying, and Aunt Beck said, "Oh, no! You must be wrong! Not Lanita!"

I wanted to crawl underground and never emerge. That's when I realized that my desire to be popular had overcome my good judgment and what I'd been taught in a Christian home.

Wanting to fit in and be accepted is a natural human trait! Let's face it, we all like to be liked, whatever we might say to the contrary. We love to have friends who want to be around us. But we must not give up our Christian standards in exchange for popularity.

When I went to college, I determined that I was going to maintain the standards I'd been taught by my parents and other mentors. I discovered that at first it was a pretty lonely road to walk. But I started watching and listening to others to see what they were like. I reached out in friendship to those people and eventually I found friends with common values and matching goals. I also discovered that by being discriminating in the people I hung out with, I had true friends who would not talk about me behind my back, desert me when I was having a hard time, or dump me to be with a more popular person. And that decision I never regretted.

Dear Me in Ten Years

So how is life?
How far have you gotten?
Do you like yourself?
Do you like what you doing?
Career wise
Do you have a boyfriend/girlfriend?
Is he treating you like a man and not a boy?
Is she loving you they way the Shulamite loves her beloved
Are you married?
Do you have kids?
Are you happy?
How's mom and dad?
How is that little brother of yours?
Are still sane?
Do you know who you are?
Or are you lost in the world
Is God still in your life?
Do you still believe?
Do you still want to help people?
Do you stand around waiting for things to happen?
Or go and explore the depths of the unknown
Do you still care?
Or are you numb
Are you still that same boy or girl that people once knew?
Or just another person lost in themselves, not really knowing what
the heck is going on
Again are you happy?
Truly
Call mom she can help you
If not
God is always there
Always

Love Completely

And he said to him, "You shall love the Lord your God with all your heart and with all your soul and with all your mind." Matthew 22:37 ESV

When asked which was the greatest of all the commandments, this was Jesus' response.

This truth takes a fraction of a second to read and an eternity to perfect.

Just what can a busy college student – or any of us – do to love the Lord completely?

How can we love Him with all our heart?

How can we love Him with all our soul?

And how can we love Him with all our mind?

The heart...the seat of all our emotion. The Bible instructs us in Proverbs 4:23 to "keep your heart with all vigilance, for from it flow the springs of life." With all vigilance. Those are powerful words. We must read God's Word and learn what is right and true. When our heart strays from these truths – and it will – we must ask Him to enable us to "keep our heart." Every part of it is to belong to Him. "Love the Lord . . . with all your heart."

Our soul...This is our spiritual being. At times, especially when we're furthering our education, we may doubt that we have a spirit. It can't be tested in the laboratory. It can't be dissected in anatomy class. It can't be observed even using a high-powered microscope. But it's real. And without tending to our spiritual health through Bible study, prayer, and fellowship with other believers, we will not be able to love the Lord with it at all.

Last, but truly not least, we are to love the Lord with all our mind. About now you may be feeling that you can't fit one more thing into your overflowing brain, but if you don't, you won't be able to obey the Lord's command in 2 Corinthians 10:5 to "take every thought captive to obey Christ."

Like every directive in the Scriptures we can't love the Lord completely, with our entirety, unless we do so by the power of His Holy Spirit.

May we all commit to love Him more day by day.

Conflict: Wise Up, Humble Down

Jealousy and selfishness cause fights. Period. James 4:1-3 NLT clearly states this: "What is causing the quarrels and fights among you?....You are jealous of what others have, but you can't get it....you want only what will give you pleasure."

How can you apply these verses to periods of conflict in your life? I can relate when I reminisce about an "unjust" parking ticket, a silent treatment between my roommate and me over a bathroom trashcan, breaking a "no shorts" dress code during the 100 plus degree summer at my conservative Christian university, or the lecture from my parents about working and finances.

Whatever the conflict, evil desires were at war (James 4:1 NLT). So how do we handle this conflict especially in a time of self-exploration and independence seeking that occurs during college?

1. Humble yourself
2. Become a peacemaker
3. Ask for wisdom.

According to James, brother of Jesus, not only does God favor humility, He honors it. How can you show humility or an extra measure of mercy to your roommate? To a classmate during a group project?

Be a peacemaker. Proverbs 19:11 NLT says, "A person's insight gives him patience, and his virtue is to overlook an offense." God promises peace, strength, and courage (just check out some Old Testament stories about Gideon or David). He promises peace even when we feel insignificant or when the problems we face are huge. Perhaps the best way to manage being a peacemaker is to ask for wisdom. "If you need wisdom, ask our generous God, and he will give it to you." James 1:5 NLT. As peacemakers and humble followers of Jesus, it is not necessary to fight your way to the top of your class, the top of an argument, the top of your dorm, the top of your profession, or the top of your fraternity/sorority/social club. Ask for wisdom, and receive it with a heart willing to leave evil desires such as jealousy and selfishness behind on the cross.

Moment By Moment

Alarm clocks sound. A new day.

Coffee perks. A new awakening.

Showers rain down. A new cleansing.

Scripture read. A new understanding.

Classes are calling. Papers need writing. Tests need answers.

Each of these moments are calling you.

Each moment will arrive and dissolve.

Whether good or bad, every single moment is an ending and new beginning.

Today you will have a choice to set God's kingdom in motion here on earth. What will you do with the moments from your day? Come humbly into the presence of the Lord today and greet Him with thanksgiving for each moment. Pray today that each earthly moments can and will be used for eternity. Pray that in the moments ahead you will remember Micah 6:8: seek justice, love mercy, and walk humbly with your Father.

Thank you Lord for each moment.

Thank you Lord for preparing an eternal Heaven, which will be filled with perfect moments, perfect love and intimacy with you.

Run Your Race

In 1998 I completed the New York City Marathon. I was not the first one to cross the finish line. The race officials did not declare me the winner. In fact I finished 19,354th. I was well back in the pack even among my own age group. However, what was interesting about the apparent non-eventful completion of the race was that I was the only one of the 40,000 plus participants with my name. So the reality was, I did finish first in the category of "me."

When I crossed the finish line 4 hours and 13 minutes after the starter's gun sounded, the course attendants placed around my neck the exact same medal received by those who ran sub-two hour races. You see, it was really not about where I finished but that I did. The shiny, bronze-tinted medal was a nice award, but it could never represent the real-time hours of preparation it took to actually get to the finish line in Central Park. The reward for finishing was the same for all who completed the course successfully. But for me the tangible prize was only a representation and culmination of what I had learned and experienced throughout the process of preparing for the event.

Paul says it this way in his first letter to the Corinthians, "Do you not know that those who run in a race all run, but only one receives the prize? Run in such a way that you may win. Everyone who competes in the games exercises self-control in all things. They then do it to receive a perishable wreath, but we an imperishable. Therefore, I run in such a way, as not without aim; I box in such a way, as not beating the air; but I discipline my body and make it my slave, so that, after I have preached to others, I myself will not be disqualified." (1 Corinthians 9:24-27 NASB)

As you look ahead to what God has in store for you, remember, you are not only competing against those running the same race but against being the best "you" you can be. How was I able to make it to the finish line? By preparing with a purpose. By being disciplined with determination. By persevering through pain when things became difficult. For what prize are you running? Is it a perishable or imperishable one?

Taking the Detours

In their hearts humans plan their course, but the Lord directs their steps.
Proverbs 16:9 NIV

After 10 years of study, I landed my dream job teaching psychology at a regional university. I knew that God was intimately involved in my appointment because the woman who had just vacated the position told me she'd been praying for a Christian to take her place. At the end of my first year, I was promoted and received tenure. That meant I could stay in that job for the rest of my working life. I also had the opportunity to do a little campus ministry on the side, so I felt I was having some impact for Christ. My career was set. The only problem was that God had other plans.

After a few years, I felt God prompting me to resign and do some unpaid study and field assignments with a Christian mission organization. Some of my closest friends and family thought I was crazy. 'Why don't you just ask for leave?' Their arguments made perfect sense and it was tempting to heed their advice. It was hard to go against others and give up everything I'd known, but I couldn't escape the fact that God wanted me to leave my secure well-paid job and step out into an uncertain future.

I wrote my letter of resignation and handed it to my boss. By the time I left his office, he had granted me 20 months leave without pay. God had provided a safety net without me asking for it. I was amazed at his provision, though I wasn't expecting to return. Again, God had different plans. After three courses and two overseas mission projects, God led me back to my job at a secular university where I was able to implement a new class on religious issues in counseling. The class ran for five years and provided a forum for discussing many Christian topics, an opportunity that wouldn't have been possible without the teaching and experiences I'd gained during my time away.

God uses people in all vocations to reach others for Him, but always be open to his promptings and detours. He sees the big picture and has a reason for sending you down those roads. You may have chosen your course of study, but He's the one who ultimately directs your path.

What Are You Hanging On To?

It was not you who sent me here, but God. Genesis 45:8 NIV

"God's plans are better than your dreams!"

1610 Likes for the chaplain's Facebook status. A young woman's comment caught my eye: "But wouldn't god have given u those dreams in the first place??"

Joseph thought so. Genesis 37:5-46:4 describes his dream story – of fantastical dreams concerning his future. What happens when Joseph shares them? He's sold into slavery and a world of strife! Sure, time eventually proves that Joseph's dreams were God-given. But not every dream comes from God, no matter how good it seems. Hanging on to the wrong dream can cause even more strife.

To assume our own desires and dreams are God-given leaves us vulnerable to a whole gambit of grief if they fail. I know. I've been there. When my dream crashed, I became discouraged, depressed, angry at the world and at God. He wasn't at fault; my expectations were. It's hard to relinquish a dream, especially one we thought came from God. But I've discovered it's far more satisfying, fulfilling, and joy-giving to release a dream in order to hang on to God, than to let go of God to hang on to a dream.

Trusting that God's plans are better than ours and resting in His unfailing ability to work them out, gives us incredible peace and God incredible freedom to work his brilliant plans out in us and through us – even when prospects look disastrous. I doubt Joseph dreamed of languishing in an Egyptian prison, though it fit God's plan. Joseph's dream-come-true rested outside of his circumstances or control.

Some argue that God's plans only work out if we obey him. I'm all for obedience, (great reward program!), but guess what – sometimes, despite our best intentions, we stuff up. That is where God's infinite grace and mercy abound. His love is so great that he works for our good, even when we miss the mark or mistake our dream for God's plan.

Are you uncertain of, or discouraged about, your elusive dream? Wondering if God's forgotten you? Or your dream? Release the dream. Hang on to God because, "we know that in all things God works for the good of those who love him, who have been called according to his purpose" (Romans 8:28).

Be Yourself

By the grace of God I am what I am, and his grace toward me has not been in vain. On the contrary I worked harder than any of them – though it was not I, but the grace of God that is with me. Whether then it was I or they, so we proclaim and so you have come to believe.
1 Corinthians 15:10-11 NRSV

When I was younger and new in the faith I wanted people to know who I was and what I believed – so desperately that I tripped over my own two feet. It somehow eluded me that I only had to be who I really am, and put my best foot forward. What you see is what you get.

It's difficult when you meet a new group of peers for the first time. They all look so cool and confident that you just know it's going to be difficult to be yourself and fit in. But that is all you have to do – just be yourself. Relax and go with the flow.

As a denominational editor for 24 years I travelled across Canada and North America and to many foreign countries. In some countries Christians were not welcome and even prohibited from expressing their beliefs. I met with people of varying backgrounds, peasants and heads of state; people of all faiths and many colors of skin. I always allowed my Christian background to come through in what I said or did but I never imposed it on others or tried to proselytize them. If the subject came up I acknowledged my faith and expressed what I believed. People seemed to respect my position and felt free to express their own religious beliefs.

Through the years I have been surprised by colleagues and acquaintances who have come to me and said, "You are a Christian, aren't you? Tell me about it." It has been my joy to share openly about my Lord and Saviour.

Know that God is always with you and that you are a living expression of God in your life, wherever you go and whoever you are with. People will respect you for what you believe and at times seek you out to help them understand about faith. Invite them as they seem willing to share some of what you believe. Slow and steady wins the race.

Reconciliation First

Therefore, if you are offering your gift at the altar and there remember that your brother has something against you, leave your gift there in front of the altar. First go and be reconciled to your brother; then come and offer your gift. Matthew 5:23-24 NIV

I couldn't sing. The praise band was rocking up front, but my mind wasn't on worship. I was standing with my hands raised along with the other 500 college students that had come out for mid-week worship. I mouthed the words, but my emotions were still churning over the fight I'd had with my roommate. I wanted to stay, but I could hear the Lord speaking to me: Go make it right.

Jesus expects us to take relationships seriously. In the Sermon on the Mount Jesus told his disciples "when you are offering your gift at the altar, if you remember that your brother or sister has something against you, leave your gift there before the altar and go; first be reconciled to brother or sister, and then come and offer your gift." Jesus first preached this sermon to a crowd of followers in Galilee, almost 70 miles from Jerusalem. Was Jesus really suggesting that if a disciple was offering a lamb at the temple and remembered that he had somehow offended another disciple, he or she should leave his lamb there at the temple, make the three day journey home, reconcile the relationship, and only then return to the temple? Maybe not. Perhaps here, as Jesus does elsewhere, he was using exaggeration to make his point (Matthew 5:29-30). But the principle holds: there is no room for lack of reconciliation in the body of Christ.

We know that we are supposed to forgive others. But the burden is also on us to take initiative in being reconciled when we are the ones who have offended or wounded other people. It's hard to admit we're wrong. It's humbling to say we're sorry. But we can't worship God and hurt others at the same time. Faith is meant to be lived in community, and pursuing peace with God means pursuing peace with others as well. It is our duty to humble ourselves, ask forgiveness, and be reconciled. Reconciliation can't wait.

Books or Food

And when you pray, do not keep on babbling like pagans, for they think they will be heard because of their many words. Do not be like them, for your Father knows what you need before you ask him. Matthew 6:8 NIV

How am I going to afford textbooks? Today I must make a decision. How can I tell that God will provide for me? He did when Jesus was on earth.

True, things have changed even since my experiences of college in America. We had two children and because we were foreign students, I was not allowed to work for pay. My husband worked for the university part-time as an office-equipment technician in the days before everyone had computers. He would give me money for groceries and then need more textbooks, so I would have to give it back. I was fearful and wondered how we would feed ourselves. In spite of my fears, God knew of our needs and without our asking for help, generous people would leave groceries at our door or leave money in an envelope. Sometimes I would do things for people and they would insist on giving me a donation.

What do you have to buy right now? I have learned to write it down, then when God provides, I am able to thank Him and tell my story later in life.

Only the Lonely

*The time is coming, and is already here, when all of you will be scattered,
each of you to your own home, and I will be left all alone. But I am not
really alone, because the Father is with me. John 16:32, GNT*

I lived at home during my college years, but many of my closest
friends were out-of-town students who lived in the dorms. After four
years, we finished our undergraduate training and my friends moved
away. The first couple of months were really difficult for me. I missed
them so much. We'd still keep in touch by phone (this was in the days
before texting, email and Skype), but that couldn't compare to seeing
them in person, laughing together, and being able to give each other
a hug.

One day when I was feeling particularly lonely, I glanced at the Bible
sitting on my desk. I knew I should give my concerns to God, but my
heart wasn't in it. Reading scripture might help a little, but it wouldn't
ease the longing I had for my friends. I reluctantly picked up my Bible
and opened it at random. My eyes immediately fell on the verse above:
'all of you will be scattered, each of you to your own home, and I will
be left all alone.' That's exactly what had happened to me. 'But I am
not really alone, because the Father is with me.'

That verse surged through me like a lightning bolt and I burst into
tears. I could hardly believe that God loved me so much He would speak
directly to my need at that very moment. When Jesus said those words,
He was prophesying about how the disciples would desert him after his
arrest in the Garden of Gethsemane. My friends hadn't abandoned me
on purpose, but I certainly felt the emptiness caused by their leaving.
Jesus had been there. He understood my loneliness.

In the weeks and months that followed, God brought many wonderful new friends into my life. He cheered me in a very tangible way,
but I never forgot that verse.

Perhaps you're feeling lonely today. Trust God with your circumstances and He will fill the void in your life in ways you can't even
imagine. He's with you now and will never leave you. That's a promise
you can bank on.

Is Anybody There?

Ever been to a party, event or activity among a group of people, yet felt totally alone and wonder, is anybody there? How is it you can be surrounded by classmates, friends and roommates yet still have feelings of loneliness, or isolation? Faces pass you in the hallways, the sounds of laughter, music, and arguing, let you know that are others are within your reach, yet you ask yourself, is anybody there?

Being amid your peers at a career fair, during final exams, or even at commencement exercises, doesn't necessarily mean you don't feel alone and you may ask, is anybody there? Daunting thoughts of job searches, returning home or moving away, along with an uncertain future, can make you feel alone and wonder 'is anybody there? How can I do all this alone and by myself?'

Well, wait a minute, at times like these, stop for a second, and close your eyes and focus. Ask the question again, is anybody there? Is anybody really there? Now listen, listen carefully.

Of course there is! Sure there is somebody! You are not alone, you are never alone. Have you forgotten: "Be determined and confident. Do not be afraid of them. Your God, the Lord himself, will be with you. He will not fail you or abandon you." Deuteronomy 31:6 GNT

Have faith, because He will never abandon you or leave you alone. You may feel alone at times but you are not alone, you are never alone, He is with you always! Trust in Him as he will guide you on your life's journey. Together with Him you can never be alone.

Is anybody there?

God is there.

Lean On Your Faith

Inspired by the life of Joseph in the Book of Genesis

A dreamer of dreams often referenced of him
This dreamer was captured by their jealousy and sin
Majority vote–and Joseph was tossed in to a hole
For twenty pieces of silver by his brothers, was sold
Separated from family and the brother he loved
Completely depended on the Father above
Leaned on his faith and the Keeper of life
Relied on God's promises while surrounded by strife
Though temptation and doubt surely came his way
He maintained his integrity and sought time to pray
Lived life by example, diligently spoke truth
Stood firm on his faith in the God of his youth
Joseph's life – it was planned by the Lord God above
Same for you and for me, then sealed with His love
So no matter what fate may come your way
Whether blessing or sorrow, you must lean on your faith!

Looking for Wisdom

It's been a long time since I was in college, but as someone who became a Christian during my freshman year at a Big 10 school, I still remember how spiritual things came alive to me once I trusted Christ as my savior. My sweet roommate, Martha, led me to the Lord. I wanted to read my Bible all the time. I was so excited to know more and more about Jesus and to understand this new mystery. There was no Internet in those days so I couldn't just Google topics I was interested in, but Martha had an amazing little bookcase with a wealth of Christian books.

One author I was especially drawn to was Catherine Marshall. Through her writing I learned how a life of faith fit into my everyday life. She taught me principles, drawn from the Bible for sure, but made even more compelling and understandable by the way she wove them throughout the stories from her life. It was from her that I learned about the concept of praise as a sacrifice and about the sovereignty of God in everything that touches our lives.

Years later, I continue to read my Bible, and I also continue to read Christian authors, even revisiting my Catherine Marshall books. A word of caution… be discerning and measure everything you read and hear against Scripture. Never neglect your Bible, but also learn from others' experiences and the things God has revealed to them. Read old authors and read new authors and make your walk richer and your path smoother by gleaning from their wisdom. Learn through the eyes of your Christian brothers and sisters, stay on the path the Lord has set before you, and you'll be better equipped to honor God with your life and offer counsel and truth to anyone who comes to you.

Without counsel plans fail, but with many counselors they succeed.
Proverbs 15:22 ESV

Help God....I got an F

Help God, I got an F on my exam today. I was not being tested on mathematical equations, scientific theories, or historical facts. I was tested in the area of forgiveness. It's the person I least expected, the one who is the closest to me that broke my trust. How do I genuinely forgive this person?

Peter, one of Jesus' closest friends, struggled with forgiving others. In Matthew 18:21-22 (NIV) he poses an important question, one that must have troubled him on many occasions. He asked Jesus, "How many times should I forgive my brother or sister who offends me?" Peter, like many of us, placed a limit by stating that seven times should be sufficient. Surely forgiving someone this many times is an act of kindness.

Jesus' reply to Peter must have taken him by surprise. He said that Peter should forgive "not seven times, but seventy times seven." What a thought provoking statement! Jesus understood Peter and did not condemn him for asking this question. He realized that forgiveness does not come naturally. It is a virtue, a character trait that comes from God.

Perhaps like Peter, you too are struggling to forgive someone close to you. You may be saying, "You don't know what they did to me, you don't understand." Hebrews 4:15 says, "For we do not have a high priest who is unable to empathize with our weaknesses, but we have one who has been tempted in every way, just as we are —yet He did not sin." God understands and is able to help you work through your challenges to forgive. Below are a few practical steps to help.

Identify the real reason you are struggling to forgive the other person. Name the offense.

Be open and honest with God. Pour your heart out to the Lord in prayer regarding it.

Relinquish your sense of entitlement to punish the person who did wrong.

Believe that God cares and that He is a righteous judge. He will handle any issue where there is an injustice. You can trust Him to take care of it.

Take a moment to reflect upon what changes you can expect to see in your life when you choose to forgive someone.

First Impression, Second Chance

*Praise the Lord, O my soul; all my inmost being, praise His holy Name.
Praise the Lord, O my soul, and forget not all His benefits-who forgives
all your sins and heals all your diseases, who redeems your life from the pit
and crowns you with love and compassion. He does not treat us as our sins
deserve or repay us according to our iniquities. For as high as the heavens
are above the earth,so great is His love for those who fear Him.*
Psalm 103:1-4, 10-11 NIV

When I first met Mike, our regional boss, I strongly disliked him.
He seemed haughty, arrogant, and intimidating. I tried to avoid him
whenever possible.

My supervisor, sensing my frustration, tried to offer encouragement.
I rejected it, but God had a lesson in store for me.

I had worked late. The day had been a series of disasters, and I still
had to help with our annual residents' Thanksgiving dinner. I didn't
want to help, and I definitely didn't want Mike around. I just wanted
to go home. I sat at my desk, feeling sorry for myself and hoping Mike
would leave. Instead of leaving, he put down his belongings, came over
to my desk and asked, "Are you depressed today?"

I replied, "Yeah, Mike. I am." To my surprise, he was genuinely
concerned. Although he'd worked as many hours as I had, Mike took
time to talk with me, encourage me, and get my focus back on the Lord.

As we talked, God showed me that Mike wasn't the "meanie" I
thought I knew. What I had perceived as meanness was simply Mike's
conscientiousness about our work and our elderly residents' quality of
care. A positive relationship resulted because God turned a bad first
impression into a blessed second chance.

Is there someone in your life today who made a bad first impression
on you? Perhaps it's one of your professors, a co-worker, or even your
roommate. Ask the Lord to help you see that person through His eyes.
Look for something positive about him or her, and most of all, keep that
person in your prayers. God can do amazing things with second chances.

Living in Tornado Alley

When you pass through the waters, I will be with you; and when you pass through the rivers, they will not sweep over you. When you walk through the fire, you will not be burned; the flames will not set you ablaze.
Isaiah 43:2 NIV

You have arrived at college. Your bags are unpacked and then a siren blares. Is this for real or a false alarm?

It was only two weeks after I had arrived in Tulsa, Oklahoma from New Zealand. Our two children were safely tucked in bed. The sky had been looking like upside down ice-cream cones during the day and no birds were flying around. The wind started to rise and torrential rain hammered on the roof. I looked out the window of our bedroom and saw small trees bent almost to the ground. As the wind howled and the little cottage shook, I took a promise from my promise box and read from Isaiah 43:2. Somehow, we were going to be safe.

The next morning we went outside and found huge cottonwood tree branches had been blown clear over where we were living. There was not even a branch or twig for at least ten feet out all round the cottage. Just down the street, a branch had fallen onto someone's roof. We had not yet learned what to do when storms struck in Tulsa. The one thing we knew was that God was with us no matter what happened.

Home Away from Home

For He Himself has said, "I will never leave you nor forsake you."
Hebrews 13:5 NKJV

Last year, my sister and I had to make the difficult decision of moving our mother into a long-term skilled nursing care center. Mom made it a little easier for us by recognizing and accepting that she needed more care and supervision than her family could provide. The hardest part for my mom was adapting to living with a roommate. The adjustment of leaving your own home and all that is familiar is daunting enough. It can be frightening to suddenly find yourself living in a small room with a complete stranger! Her first two roommates did not work out. But the center is diligent in finding each resident a compatible roommate and my mom and Betty are now "roomies." They do not agree on everything and probably get a bit annoyed with each other at times. But they are able to live together in one room. They look out for each other, share laughs and concerns, and have become friends.

Watching my mom adjust to her new surroundings and sharing living quarters brought to mind the year I lived in a dorm while attending nursing school. I remember that first night away from the familiar, safe place I called "home." I felt abandoned, alone, separated from all that was comfortable. I remember feeling discouraged when my first roommate and I were not the least compatible. But, like the nursing center, the school worked at getting the right combination in roommates. I decided to give it a chance and my second roommate and I got along well. I was able to adapt to dorm life and group living.

I was never alone even though it seemed like it those first few weeks. God never leaves us alone. He has given us His Spirit to walk beside us and surrounds us with others who will provide encouragement and support. Perhaps you are struggling to adjust to new living quarters like a dormitory or nursing care center. Even a short stay in the hospital or a rehabilitation center can be unsettling. Whenever you feel alone, remember that God has promised to always be your "roommate"!

God is our refuge and strength, a very present help in trouble.
Psalm 46:1 NKJV

The Traveler

And the Word became flesh, and dwelt among us, and we saw His glory,
glory as of the only begotten from the Father, full of grace and truth.
John 1:14 NAS

He, too, left His home which was familiar, good, and beautiful,
entered a country where so much seemed so strange.
Even though He spoke their language,
they couldn't seem to understand Him,
    and so, He talked it over with his Father.
He, too, joined the residents in everyday activities;
He did some carpentry, went to a wedding, broke up a funeral.
He even walked the shoreline,
doing His unconventional style of "fishing,"
    and all the while, He talked it over with His Father.
He, too, made some good friends, and shared with them
His Good News, knowing that His time with them was short.
Then when all He'd come to do was done,
He promised He would never leave them nor forsake them,
until that day He'd come to take them Home—
    to Father.

Father, I want those you have given me to be with me where I am, and to
see my glory. John 17:24a NIV

Voices

See to it that no one takes you captive through hollow and deceptive philosophy, which depends on human tradition and the basic principles of this world rather than on Christ. Colossians 2:8 NIV

After two years of secretarial school, I decided to hit the mainstream of full-time employment. Always desiring to be a school teacher, I married a wonderful man that helped my dream become reality. Although I was older attending classes, I still met with adverse opinions regarding my faith in Jesus Christ. I felt well versed in what I believed and how to present evidence of that belief, but being older didn't mean I was exempt from fielding tough questions. In fact, I encountered one professor who was determined to change my thinking on the subject of evolution.

Dr. Brown (name changed) took every opportunity to challenge my faith. On one particular encounter Dr. Brown requested students meet with him individually mid-semester. During that encounter he began challenging my stance on evolution vs. creation again. As he prodded, I finally said, "Dr. Brown, I think we've come to an impasse on this subject. If evolution was successful, why do we still have apes and monkeys today?" Dr. Brown looked puzzled as I forged ahead.

"Tell you what, Dr. Brown. Until we can bring a monkey into this office, place him into a cage and watch him evolve over the next couple of years, I just don't see how this idea of yours can be founded." At this, the professor smiled and never mentioned the subject to me again. My answer might have been simplistic, but it brought home my point.

I continue to believe the Holy Spirit entered that room and gave me the courage and the answer needed at the time. My point is simple; live your faith one day at a time. Pray fervently that the Holy Spirit will provide words wrapped in truth as you are confronted or questioned. Never back down from an opportunity to be a witness. You are a child of the Most High God. He is the truth and is willing to grant us wisdom and knowledge when we call on His Name.

Father, Guard the hearts and minds of these students against "the basic principles of this world." May they become strong Christian believers and bring others to know Christ. In Jesus' name. Amen!

Going to the World

"What if I get motion sickness? Are you going to help me pack? What if I'm not up to handling the taxing conditions, heat, and humidity? What must I do when I go through security and customs? How much can my bag weigh?"

All questions my mother had before leaving on a mission trip to Jamaica. But God provided the answers. She took motion sickness pills before boarding. My wife and I showed her how to properly pack her bags and condiments. A family friend paid for her plane ticket and accommodations. A church group provided funds for purchasing VBS supplies. The resort chefs hosted a buffet even though the group was late returning, and two men safely maneuvered the un-air-conditioned buses around potholes and over rough and narrow mountain terrain.

God provided—as he always does and always will. Therefore, go and make disciples of all the nations, baptizing them in the name of the Father and the Son and the Holy Spirit (Matthew 28:19 NLT).

Regardless of how we go, God will forever go with us through the person and power of his Spirit residing in us. And the methods by which we can go are every changing and increasing. I was reminded of this recently when I befriended a lady on the other side of the world through a Facebook group. As we talked about E-readers and apps, she said, "I have a word from God. He will use these...to get his Word out to the nations."

So whether you're telling the message by hitting the enter key, the post button, or the send key, by being kind to a neighbor, or by sharing with a fellow student what God's done in your life, just go to the nations. And however you go, God will go with you.

Prayer: Prompt us Merciful Father, to take Your love to the nations by using every available means.

Nothing But Christ

For my part, I am going to boast about nothing but the Cross of our Master, Jesus Christ. Because of that Cross, I have been crucified in relation to the world, set free from the stifling atmosphere of pleasing others and fitting into the little patterns that they dictate. Galatians 6:14 Message

In a
Times Square
Powerball
MTV
James Bond
Justin Beiber
iPhone
Disney and
Dubai
kind of world,
let nothing
but Christ
dazzle you.

"Apart from Him, let nothing dazzle you" – Ignatius of Loyola

Through the Planner's Eyes

We humans keep brainstorming options and plans, but God's purpose prevails. Proverbs 19:21 Message

Would you consider yourself a planner? Perhaps as you considered which colleges to apply to you imagined yourself in your dream job, with your dream car, in your dream condo and made plans to associate with certain people or take certain classes to arrive at your planned destination.

I have friends who are big planners. From the time they were freshmen in high school, they carefully considered each step of their life. They knew what school they wanted to go to, where they wanted to live when they graduated from college, what career path they wanted to pursue, even when and how many kids they wanted to have, and where they wanted to settle in their retirement years. It's like they had their life's check off list: School – check; Job – check; Spouse – check; Kids – check.

I'm not suggesting that making plans are bad. All too often we make our own plans not including God in the planning process or we ask Him to bless them once we've made them. I know God has a plan for our lives. Jeremiah 29:11 (LB) says "For I know the plans I have for you, says the Lord. They are plans for good and not for evil, to give you a future and a hope."

We can make all kinds of plans yet, Proverbs 19:21 is clear, only those plans which God makes will succeed.

As I thought about this verse, I couldn't help but think about Mary's plan. Engaged to be married, I'm sure Mary planned for her future with Joseph. After married they'd start a family. Yes, she would become a mother, but God's plan was much bigger. She would give birth to His one and only Son who would one day save the entire world from the grip of death. I don't know about you, but I'm not convinced she planned for that…how could she really?

God's plans are so much bigger than we can ever dare to dream or imagine. He wants the very best for us, a prosperous future, and an eternal home. Does this mean we shouldn't plan? NO. We should plan we just need to include God in our planning process.

What are you planning that you haven't talked to Him about yet? Remember NOTHING is too small.

College Game Plan

Call to me and I will answer you and tell you great and unsearchable things you do not know. Jeremiah 33:3 NIV

When I left for college, someone advised: "Study as if you didn't pray, and pray as if you didn't study." I took this counsel to heart and made it my college game plan.

As an undergraduate and later as a graduate student, I studied hard and prayed hard. God helped me to complete my courses and graduate with honors. Study + prayer added up to a winning combination.

You've probably received lots of study tips. Here are a few suggestions for prayer:

While you study:
- Lord, help me understand this course.
- Guide me as I study, and help me master the important information.

Before exams:
- Lord, help me study the right material so I'm prepared for the exam.
- Please help me recall what I've learned and do my best on the test.

During exams:
- Lord, help me explain my answers clearly to demonstrate what I know.
- Lord, I'm not sure which is the right answer; help me choose the correct one.

After exams:
- Lord, help the grader to understand my answers; give me favor.
- I pray for a fair grade and the ability to accept the outcome.

Whether or not you have a test coming up, keep praying. God loves to hear from you—both with requests and with thanks for His answers. He wants to be a member of your team and help you have a winning college season.

Lord, thank You for helping me in college. I want to team up with You and please You in all I do. Help me take time not only to study for classes but also to read the most important textbook—the Bible—to learn more about You. In Jesus' name. Amen.

The Smorgasbord of Freedom

You should know that your body is a temple for the Holy Spirit who is in you. You have received the Holy Spirit from God. So you do not belong to yourselves, because you were bought by God for a price. So honor God with your bodies. 1 Corinthians 6:19-20 NCV

Growing up in a very conservative Baptist home, my Dad was very protective to say the least. His protection included monitoring my friends, destinations, activities and dates. It became a world of "don'ts" with very few "dos" where I felt not only stifled, but unable to be trusted in making positive decisions.

Since I attended a local community college and lived at home, I decided to see what was so wrong about all those "don'ts" when I moved out on my own. I could probably write several pages on my choices and their awry outcomes. But I did discover an understanding of why my dad had taken a firm approach as the guardian of my life. His desire was to impact and shape my future decisions.

Why do I relay this message to college-aged students? To share the fact that there will be, if there hasn't already, an invitation for you to join the majority of young people at the smorgasbord of freedom. You will be the deciding factor in what you do, with whom you associate, the activities you will be involved in, how much studying you decide to do and if you will be successful in attaining the degree for which you are attending your said college.

However, nothing can be accomplished or give peace to you apart from the Lord Jesus. Jesus is our Shepherd and He is available 24/7 to meet any and all needs you encounter throughout these college years and beyond. There are Christian groups on college campuses that sponsor activities and weekly gatherings that would be to your advantage. Students that are involved in these groups will help hold you accountable to a lifestyle that is honoring to the Lord.

Give honor and glory to the Lord, my young friends. He'll never leave you or forsake you.

Father, I ask that you watch over, guard and protect the reader of this devotional. Lord, please give discernment in decisions and wisdom when confronted with issues against your commands. May friendships be found that are honoring to Jesus. In Jesus' name. Amen.

Choices

Our world is filled with a culture and lifestyle that is not honoring, good, or pleasing in the sight of the Lord. Does God look at the world He created and speak the same words He once spoke in Genesis 6? Does He regret making us? Is His heart broken and deeply troubled once again? God created us to bring Him honor, glory, and pleasure. Anything we say or do that doesn't fulfill those goals must make His heart hurt. In Genesis 6, we see that God regretted making humans and was deeply troubled because every thought and deed was evil. But Noah stood out and against what the world said was good. He found favor in God's eyes. When the world said one thing, Noah set himself apart.

How did Noah find favor in God's eyes? He was righteous. He chose right living. He made choices that were good, true, pure, and admirable. He stood against the world. He was blameless. His heart was pure. That doesn't mean he wasn't sinful. But he was free of guilt because he walked faithfully with God. There is a difference between living and making good choices and walking faithfully with God.

Noah sought God's approval above man's. Will you step out and against what the world says is good? Will you find favor in God's eyes with your choices? Choose what is good. Walk faithfully with God. Bring God pleasure.

Prayer: Open my eyes LORD to see the world as You see it. Open my eyes to what I thought was good that has been twisted enough to appear good, but is really sin. Break my heart for what breaks Yours. Move me to stand up for what is right and good and perfect. Help me to speak truth in love and to see the world as You created it to be. Make me sensitive to those lost in a dark world. Come LORD Jesus, Come.

Every Step of the Way

Fear not, for I am with you; Be not dismayed, for I am your God. I will strengthen you, Yes, I will help you. Isaiah 41:10 NKJV

I watched my parents pull away from the curb, waved good-bye, and choked back the tears that threatened to spill down my cheeks. My churning insides reflected a level of anxiety I had not anticipated as a high school senior choosing a college 825 miles from home. What had I been thinking?

Wandering back to my dorm, I tried to pull myself together. I didn't know one person on this campus before I arrived. I already had a hunch my roommates would probably not be my best friends, and the Southern Tennessee culture could not have differed more from my hometown near Buffalo, New York. I felt lost.

My mom's reminder elbowed its way into my thoughts "A man who has friends must himself be friendly" (Proverbs 18:24).

"Oh, Lord, please help me. I'm not very outgoing. I feel so overwhelmed..."

I learned something those first few days and weeks. A smile goes a long way. I learned to take initiative and introduce myself. I found I wasn't the only one feeling new and awkward. And I met some students from much farther away than I, even a few from other countries. The routine of classes helped—in spite of feeling inundated with class requirements. At least my feet had somewhere to go and my hands had something to do.

As the semester progressed, I learned something else. I was never alone. Oh, I knew all about God's presence growing up, but now His Word became alive to me in a personal way. Before my arrival, I never needed God *this* much. But here, I had to ask for grace as I tried to navigate so many changes. When I read God's promises, I found myself saying, "I get this now."

I still don't like saying good-bye. Yet I've learned that God can always be counted on. He's dependable no matter where we are. He is with us every step of the way.

Engaging Your Core

I can do all things in him who strengthens me. Philippians 4:13 RSV

When I went to rehab after knee surgery, the physical therapist told me, "Engage your core."

I finally got up the courage to ask, "What am I supposed to engage?"

She repeated, "Engage your core."

"Could you explain in plain English what you want me to do? Then I'll try," I responded. The gist of her explanation involved drawing my belly button up and back toward my spine. As my core grew stronger, my back hurt less.

As I recovered I thought about how strength, both physical and spiritual, was related to the core of my life, Jesus is the pillar on whom I lean. Apart from him, I have no support when I meet trials. I can't overcome challenges or help friends who are going through a difficult time without engaging my faith, i.e. my spiritual core. Through prayer and the study of Scripture, I've learned that He guides me, supports me, protects me, and heals me. When I fail to engage my core, I lack the means of grace to cope with the challenges of each day.

God's Presence

My presence will go with you, and I will give you rest. Exodus 33:14 NIV

A change of direction left me coping with a busy office situation. One day sitting at a desk piled with letters and receipts, and deadlines looming, I felt God's presence in a particular way as He assured me that this was His will for me. At other times, too, as I communed with him He assured me that this was where I was needed in His programme. He was with me and continued to uphold me every moment of the day, as I rested in and trusted in Him.

Moses met with God while tending sheep near a bush on the edge of a desert (Exodus 3:1); Gideon was threshing wheat (Judges 6:12); and Elijah rested in a cave (1 Kings 19:13) when a special encounter with God occurred. Did Martha, a woman of faith, learn to quietly practise the presence of God as she "served" (John 12:2) while her sister anointed the feet of Jesus with oil and received a memorial?

You may be struggling with a situation: pressures build; piles of study may confront you; or exams may be pending. Or you may be seated or standing in a church pew pondering on life's issues while songs are sung or a message given. God can meet you wherever you are. His presence is real and intimate. The transcendent, omnipotent God who is all-powerful knows our need, and our feelings.

Comparing Yourself to Others

So since we find ourselves fashioned into all these excellently formed and marvelously functioning parts in Christ's body, let's just go ahead and be what we were made to be without enviously or pridefully comparing ourselves with each other, or trying to be something we aren't.
Romans 12:5 Message

Six-year-old Bryce was delighted to be spending time with his cousins whom he rarely saw. But it was Christmastime and Bryce and his seven older cousins were all having a good time at Grandma's house. Bryce watched fascinated as Zach, 18, and Sydney, 17, matched their skills in seeing who could do the most push ups. "Fifty eight, fifty nine, sixty," Sydney panted and "fifty eight, fifty nine, sixty and sixty-one," Zach groaned in glee for having upped her by one. But then Mitch, Zach's younger brother, dropped to the floor and proceeded to do 63 push-ups with what seemed like little effort.

Zach huffed in exasperation.

Bryce, sensitive by nature, noticed Zach's frustration.

"Don't worry, Zach, he said. "God gives everybody different gifts," and then quickly searching for what might comfort Zach, he added, "and you have good vision!"

Through the eyes of a young child, God emphasized His truth for all ages, that day. "When they measure themselves by themselves and compare themselves with themselves, they are not wise." 2 Corinthians 10:12b (NIV). God, in His wisdom, knows that satisfaction and fulfillment with who you are can only be found in acceptance of who He made you to be. Even nature displays this truth as the following poem illustrates:

Just Be You

Never did the flashing bluebird,
Look with disdain on the wren's drab brown.
And never did the wren's sweet song,
Attempt to put the woodpecker down.
One goes across the summer sky,
With jerky dips and dives,
On wings of wind, some soar and glide,
They're all designed to fly.
Doing what they're made to do,

Soaring happily and free,
What a tribute to their Creator,
What a lesson for you and me!
Prayer: Heavenly Father, help me rejoice in the gifting of others while not forgetting to be grateful for my own. Amen.

A Royal Education

*When the queen of Sheba heard about the fame of Solomon and his
relationship to the Lord, she came to test Solomon with hard questions.
Arriving at Jerusalem with a very great caravan—with camels carrying
spices, large quantities of gold, and precious stones—she came to Solomon
and talked with him about all that she had on her mind.*
I Kings 10:1-2 NIV

Though she was royalty, and already in a position of power and
prestige, the queen of Sheba desired something else: the wisdom she
would need for a full and meaningful life. With great effort and expense
"she came from the ends of the earth to listen to Solomon" (Matthew
12:42) and to learn about God – the source of Solomon's wisdom. She
traveled many hundreds of miles by desert caravan to get from Sheba in
southern Arabia to Israel's Jerusalem, and she brought countless chests
filled with gold and precious gemstones to trade for her education.

College students today seek the best possible education they can
afford, often stretching their resources to the limit or going into debt.
Even so, college only prepares us for gainful employment; it cannot
guarantee us a full or meaningful life. For that, we need wisdom.

The surprise God has in store for us is this: we can have the wisdom
"fit for a king," for we, too, can study with Solomon! The instruction
that cost the queen so much, is available to us when we open our Bibles
to Proverbs, Song of Songs, Ecclesiastes, and Psalms 72 and 127—all
of which record Solomon's teachings. We do not have to embark on
a long, arduous, and costly journey—we just need to ask the Lord to
bless our "journey" into his Word.

Sensible people—young or old, rich or poor—are at their smartest
when they seek the best education available, and at the same time, pursue
the Lord's wisdom as taught by "Professor" Solomon.

Journey to Jerusalem

But they did not receive Him, because His face was set for the journey to Jerusalem. Luke 9:53 NKJV

The disciples had been sent ahead to prepare the way for Jesus through a Samaritan village on their journey toward Jerusalem. But the Samaritan village rejected the disciples. What was it in Jesus' countenance that caused the Samaritan village to reject him and his disciples? Luke tells us, the villagers recognized His countenance was set for the journey to Jerusalem. Having been rejected by the Jewish people for centuries, the Samaritans had grown to detest anything or anyone Jewish.

Rather than retaliate, knowing man's frailties and shortcomings, Jesus moves on. Despite James and John's desire to call down fire upon the Samaritans, Jesus rebuked them and set his face toward the next village on the journey. Jesus set his face toward his destination – Jerusalem. He kept moving forward, in spite of rejection, in spite of ridicule, in spite of threats by the religious leaders, and even in spite of well-intentioned distractions from His followers. The irony is that Jerusalem was the place of the cross. But the Apostle Mark tells us that Jesus led the way on this journey, and the disciples were both amazed and afraid (Mark 10:32).

Afraid because they had heard Jesus tell them several times by now that he would be delivered up to the cross. However, rather than retaliate against those who didn't receive him in Samaria, Jesus and the disciples moved on to the next village on their journey.

Like Jesus, we will meet rejection, we will meet ridicule, and we will meet those who don't like us. And like Jesus, we have the same opportunity to keep our face set toward our Jerusalem, our destination. The disciples momentarily forgot that Jesus and His message bring life, not death. God has not privileged us with the opportunity of belief to use it to destroy men's lives but rather to be used as His vessel in bringing salvation. But there is a cost to discipleship – a cost in the face of being mocked, ridiculed, and turned away as His disciple.

We must not look half-heartedly toward Jerusalem (heaven). God is looking for disciples who will commit themselves to the journey and to his leadership. Jesus never deterred from the plan for which God sent him. His face was set for the journey to Jerusalem in spite of all the opposition. His countenance was set to endure the cross for the joy that was set before Him (Hebrews 12:2). It is a willful act in the heart of the disciple to stay the course.

Meditation: Is your face set for the journey to Jerusalem?

Not Yet Done

"For my thoughts are not your thoughts, neither are your ways my ways,"
declares the Lord. Isaiah 55:8 NIV

When we are wronged, the natural inclination for most people is to retaliate or get even. We have the urge to "really let them have it."

"Turning the other cheek" is part of the meaning of the verse 1 Corinthians 13:5: "[Love] is not rude, it is not self-seeking, it is not easily angered, it keeps no records of wrongs."

In our human frailties we find this way of thinking difficult to follow. We not only keep a record of the wrongs, we fail to forgive. Our thinking is not like God's thoughts.

Our transformation to be made like Him is not yet complete. We are like a pancake that has only been cooked on one side—not done yet. As we grow in Christian love, His Spirit constrains us to be like Him.

Jesus had the power to annihilate all His enemies, but He did not retaliate for their cruel treatment of Him. Instead, at times, He didn't even dignify their accusations with answers.

As we allow God's Spirit to work in our hearts, we too can begin to become like Christ.

Lord, help me to forgive those who are mean and say unkind things about me as I serve you. Amen.

When Life is a Question Mark

And we know that God causes all things to work together for good to those who love God, to those who are called according to His purpose.
Romans 8:28 NASB

Of all the punctuation marks in the grammar world, which one can you most identify with as a representation of where you are on your college journey?

Periods mark the end of a statement.

Exclamation marks celebrate.

Commas are bridges to the next thing.

And question marks are waiting on an answer.

Are you at the end of a journey? Excited about a new endeavor? Ready for the next thing? Or waiting and wondering what's next?

What is the overwhelming question punctuating your life right now?

Everyone's carrying around one. We are all wondering something.

But what if we entered into the question of ourselves, giving each day a chance to change us, to make us new, and prepare us for the answer stirring inside? What if we really let our lives be lived out in fervent faith, pressing onward our prayers, and finding comfort in the questions?

Take some time today to wait and wonder and remember that creativity and beauty are found in these quiet spaces. Wherever you are in your journey, let what's punctuating your life breathe and give your marks space to do their work.

You Are Sending Me Where?

Search me, God, and know my heart; test me and know my anxious thoughts. See if there is any offensive way in me, and lead me in the way everlasting. Psalm 139:23-24 NIV

The teaching program at college offered opportunities to volunteer as a tutor for children. The assignment I was given led me to an eight-year-old boy who lived in a rough part of town. Initially my heart jumped with fear and the words that silently came to my thoughts were, "You are sending me where?"

Prayer calmed me and fearful words turned into hope, "Lord, you have given me so many blessings in life. I know you are with me everywhere I go. Now I am asked to help a child in need. Please lead me and bless this opportunity."

Happiness greeted me when I drove my car to his house and found a parking spot right in front. I took a deep cleansing breath, and knocked on the front door. "Hello, you must be Joan. Please come in and meet my son, your student Calvin." Giggles came from behind the curtain that served as a makeshift wall. The attentive father told the children to read, and keep down the noise. Calvin sat calmly at a bare oak table in the kitchen.

I spotted a basketball next to the back door. "Do you have your homework?" Calvin nodded his head, looked down, and placed a paper and a book on the table. I smiled and glanced up at his eyes. "Calvin, what do you do when you are not in school?"

Calvin looked down at the table and shrugged his shoulders. "Play ball." Addition problems were then turned into basketball games. Calvin eagerly discussed favorite games. He even laughed when I told him how I always dropped the basketball at school and wished I had a tutor for playing ball.

Anxiety left me, and now with a heart full of joy, I saw that God led me to help Calvin. Yes, His way is everlasting!

Be An Example

*Don't let anyone think less of you because you are young. Be an example to
all believers in what you say, in the way you live, in your love, your faith,
and your purity. 1 Timothy 4:12 NLT*

Living true to the faith is a challenging and ongoing process,
especially for students entering a new college environment. Perhaps for
the first time you are living away from home, leaving behind family and
friends as you embark on this new journey. During this time, different
sets of standards will rub against yours creating uncomfortable friction
between you and a friend, a roommate, or maybe even a professor. Resist
the pressure to conform to their ways that ultimately will blur better
judgement. Your steadfastness will show maturity, not immaturity as
the world would have you believe.

You don't need to be preachy. A quiet gentle spirit will speak volumes
just as effectively as a bold radical statement. Such as a respectful difference of opinion with a professor exclaims self-control. The kindness
of actions towards a struggling classmate shouts mercy. Expressing
affection to family and friends when others are watching or listening
declares courage. Refusing something that compromises beliefs states
obedience. And setting appropriate boundaries in a love-relationship
proclaims respect.

If you are fortunate to have a fellow believer come alongside you
while in college, your good conduct will help encourage that person to
stay strong as well. Those who do not share your faith will wonder why
you are so different. As stated in 1 Timothy 4:16, "Keep a close watch
on how you live and on your teaching. Stay true to what is right for the
sake of your own salvation and the salvation of those who hear you."

And don't be concerned that you are so young in years. No one will
think less of you because of your youth. They will think highly of you
because of your maturity in Christ. Live out your faith. Be an example.

Father God, I ask you to help me stay strong in my faith. Infuse
me with your strength when I feel the temptations of life threatening
to overtake me. Help me to stand for Christ whom I love and devote
myself to. Help me be an example. In Jesus' name. Amen.

No Devotion Ready

I was never involved with scouting when I was growing up. "Be Prepared" indeed! I wasn't prepared. I didn't have something up my sleeve, off the top of my head, or in reserve in any fashion. But I was asked anyway.

The request came in the form of a private message on Facebook from my niece. "Do you have a devotion you could share?" I wasn't ready for that. This was Facebook after all—the place I go to see what my daughter in California is up to. It came from the place that is my source of information on family and friends living in other parts of the country. I'm used to gleaning information from there—not having to PROVIDE it. Therein lays the problem.

I'm almost 53 years old. I've been a Christian for more than half my life. Since she asked, I am guessing my niece has a measure of respect toward me. Ask me to sing a solo….I'm ok with that. Ask me to fill in for the music director….no problem. Fill in as a Sunday School teacher and spout my mouth off….yup. But share a devotional story? My own personal feelings and observations? I don't know about that. I told her I didn't have a devotional ready. Then I began to ponder the question—and not her question but my own. Why don't I have a devotional ready?

So I studied my response to her. I told her, "I spend my days thinking about work and my evenings *not* thinking about work." So what does that response say about me? It says that I am too secluded in my own little world, even though on any given day I might come into contact with any number of the 400 fellow employees with whom I work. I might see lifelong friends out in the community. I'll spend at least a few waking hours with my bride of almost 34 years. I'll talk to my kids, my parents, and possibly my siblings. I'll hear voices coming down the hall from people in the offices near mine.

But, I don't really pay attention.

We live in a world created by the one and only true God. He has always *been* and always will *be*. He has all knowledge, all power, all wisdom, and yet, He loves me. He loves me enough that he gave His Son to die in my place. Don't ask me to give up either one of my kids for you. I might take a bullet for someone, but DO NOT ask me to put my kids in front of that same bullet. But God did! And that is why I give him my life.

So what can I do? Maybe I can start to take a little time every day and smell life's roses. Maybe I can actually start to ponder what happens daily and look to see if I can see the hand of God in it. Maybe I can spend more time in His Word and see if I hear Him speaking to me. Maybe I can try to return just a fraction of the love He has shown to me. Maybe, just maybe, I should do everything I can to fall in love again with the One Who has loved me since before there was a me to love. Maybe that's it. Do I really love Him? There is another question I should be trying to answer.

How about you? Do you really love Him? Are you looking for Him in life's victories, losses, and even daily drudgery? I'm going to open my eyes, my heart, and my mind. I'm going to invite Him to be more real in my life every day. I'm going to start paying more attention to Him. And when I do, I'm sure I'll fall more deeply in love than I have ever been before and I'll see Him, just about everywhere I look. And when I don't see Him, I'll know it's my fault and not His…because He is there…always. All I have to do is pay attention. And then I will always have a devotion ready.

Hold Fast to Your Faith

If a prophet….announces to you a sign or wonder, and if the sign or wonder spoken of takes place, and the prophet says, "Let us follow other gods" (gods you have not known) "and let us worship them," you must not listen….The Lord your God is testing you to find out whether you love him with all your heart and with all your soul. It is the Lord your God you must follow, and him you must revere. Keep his commands and obey him; serve him and hold fast to him. Deuteronomy 13:1-4 NIV

I went to my violin lesson feeling fully prepared, but it seemed my teacher expected better. She wasn't impressed that I played the right notes, or sustained each for the time count indicated in the score. She wanted to see proper bowing, confident fingering, and, worst of all, she wanted to hear expression! Then to challenge me further, she played her violin at the same time—but not in unison. She played a discordant harmony, making it even more difficult for me to hear and keep true to the proper pitch.

"I sounded much better before I came to class," I finally said, exasperated.

"No," she replied, "don't say that! It does you no good to say you played it better before coming." Seeing she had my attention, she added this punch line: "You play the music only as well as you play it under pressure. You must not let me, or what I play, distract you."

As I walked home across campus, I considered her words. They also apply to our relationship with the Lord. We can feel over-confident, or even smug about our faith in God as long as we're performing our daily routines; they are mechanical. The challenge comes when others try to introduce us to false teachings. When this happens, the steadfastness of our faith is tested. Will we remain true to Christ?

It's wise to remember this: faith is only as strong as it is under pressure.

When college, and life after college, introduces difficult "music," we want our faith to hold secure, grow strong, and produce a symphony of praise to his glory. Then we'll be able to say with joy: "My feet have closely followed his steps; I have kept to his way without turning aside" (Job 23:11).

Go With Your Gut

Your word is a lamp to my feet and a light to my path.
Psalm 119:105 NKJV

At times you will need to follow your gut instead of your peers. Many students make the mistake of caving to the pressure to follow a path that their friends are taking. But when it comes to deciding your future, only two people truly know what it is you are best suited to do, you and God. He knows what plans He has in store for you both now and in the future.

Don't follow the path that every student before you has paved or that family and friends are trying to pave for you. After all it is your path to make not someone else's. Don't let everyone else lead you astray, instead follow what you feel the Holy Spirit leading you to do.

Don't jump on the first job that offers a big paycheck when you get out of school. Money can never make a person happy. If you aren't going to enjoy pursuing a certain career, then don't do it. It may seem easier to follow the road that your family and friends paved ahead of you, but don't stray away from what God has created you to do.

It takes hard work to chase God's dreams for you, but don't give up.

Trust in the LORD with all your heart, And lean not on your own understanding; In all your ways acknowledge Him, And He shall direct your paths. Proverbs 3:5-6

A Proverb

Some things
should be told
only to God.

Gifts

Picture your eight-year-old self, opening up all your gifts on Christmas morning. You are tearing through each and every one, filling the air with ribbons, tags, and bright colored paper. You get to that last package and look around at your mess. It's over. Just like that, every single gift is open and ready to be loved.

What if God gave in that way? What if you woke up tomorrow and he gave you all the fruits of the spirit, blessed you with numerous spiritual gifts and left you with all the wisdom life had to offer?

Sounds beautiful, but honestly, I'm not sure we would know how to handle such receiving all of His gifts in one lump sum.

God's gifts are given to us in His time, in His way, for His purpose.

As our character develops, our strength is built. Strength increases faith and soon after wisdom abounds.

Think about the creative gifts God has uniquely equipped you with up to this moment. As a college student you are learning and growing and becoming the young adult God designed you to be.

Watch God use you.

Listen to His voice.

And be ready to be used, as you open up your gifts.

Finding God's Will

Speak, Lord, for your servant is listening. 1 Samuel 3:2-10 NIV

Years ago when I was due to finish college I needed to know the next step.

I had entered with a clear call from God to go to an overseas mission field. As I grew up a personal conviction had deepened. Confirmation came from the Scriptures such as "Go into all the world ..."(Mark 16:13 NIV) I felt as a pioneer missionary, maybe; but to go where the need was greatest. That's why, I, an office girl, was training in a Bible Institute.

Towards the end of the two years of Bible training, I felt a steady conviction that I should train as a nurse. So I did. I fulfilled the four years general hospital training plus an extra six months course in maternity nursing. But where was I to serve? It was not until towards the end of that period as a maternity nurse that the next step was revealed to me. I had declined an offer which I felt didn't come under "faith" principles. As I stood at the letter box into which slot I had slipped my letter of declination, into my mind crept another mission agency, and I quietly, inaudibly responded: "Yes, Lord, Why not? " Yes, why not? Indeed! I began the application process and within a few months I sailed en route to Asia.

God had kept me true to my calling. In His time he had revealed the path I was to take, and as I looked back I saw he had been leading me in that direction over the years with contacts, though I needed to wait on Him to reveal it

God guides us in different ways and at different times. It may be by a steady conviction confirmed by His written Word. Sometimes "a still small voice" is heard, quickened by taking the next step, making it known by applying or sharing the message.

In the case of the boy, Samuel, God spoke in the night, persistently, urgently, but as Samuel sought advice, and assented to listen, God spoke and revealed His plan on a leadership issue.

"Speak, Lord, for your servant is listening."

The Lord may let you wait awhile, but He *will* answer if you are intent on finding His will.

There Is a Season

For everything there is a season, a time for every activity under heaven.
Ecclesiastes 3:1 NLT

King Solomon painted a detailed backdrop in Ecclesiastes 3:1-8 of the various life seasons we will endure while on this earth. This mural depicts the beauty of life and the ugly of life, all on one canvas.

Each season has a beginning and an end. They flow from one into the next, sometimes calmly and gently, and at other times with torrential winds of change that meet our resistance.

Yet through each change of season, there is something to be learned. Times of joy and happiness teach us to remember God and praise him for his blessings. When struggles come, we may quickly turn to God for help, but often get swept away by the waves of oppression and suffering losing sight of our path. It is in these bleak seasons that we learn to persevere in the faith and depend on him. Hardships last only for a while and our God "will give a crown of beauty for ashes, a joyous blessing instead of mourning, festive praise instead of despair" (Isaiah 61:3). From out of the muck, mercies flow. If we skirt the ugly, we'll miss God's beauty. He longs to share redemption's story through each masterpiece, like you, meticulously crafted by his own hands.

What season do you find yourself in right now? Are you grieving for your family and friends? Are you struggling with grades and doubting the path you have chosen? Or are you full of excitement at the new opportunities around you? Or happy with the new relationships you are building?

If all you can muster through life's storms is a cry for help, then cry. He listens to the pleading of the brokenhearted. When you find yourself in times of contentment and joy, then praise. He delights in those who thank Him.

For everything there is a season.

Father God, may you strengthen me through the storms of life and help me depend on you. Thank you, Father, for the many blessings you have poured into my life. May you help me remember to praise you always, for all things come through your hands. In Jesus' name. Amen.

Time Management

I can do all things through Christ who strengthens me.
Philippians 4:13 NKJV

As I recited a very long list of to do's, my mind went over my options as to which things were a priority.

*study for the exam tomorrow
*start the school assignment
*walk for 45 minutes
*attend church

As I was just about to start and cut items from this very overly busy day, I turned on my computer to do my to do list. There on the front page of my web browser front and center was the following heading for an article entitled Time Management Tips That Really Work. I chuckled as I opened a blank document to write out my to do list.

As the Lord would have it, this turned out to be my to do list. He spoke to me that the best "time management" that I could do that day was to turn my focus to Him. At the end of the day it won't matter to Him what is on my list or what I got completed or didn't complete. What matters is my relationship with Him and my time spent with Him.

So now with my coffee and Bible in hand, as I go to spent time with Him before I go to church, the rest of my to do list doesn't seem so important. I am going to the Lord with my first fruits of the day.

A Buffet That Satisfies

Every part of Scripture is God-breathed and useful one way or another—
showing us truth, exposing our rebellion, correcting our mistakes, training
us to live God's way. Through the Word we are put together and shaped up
for the tasks God has for us. 2 Timothy 3:16-17 Message

A buffet meal at a restaurant is often more satisfying than a sit
down meal because there are so many delicious foods to choose from.
But to make the best selections, it's a good idea to browse along the
table and make your decisions before filling your plate. That way you
can pick the best kind of nourishment rather than overloading your
plate with poor food choices.

The same principle applies to choosing classes for college. Rather
than jumping to conclusions, study all the options available and then
narrow your choices down to those subjects that will best suit your goals.

But most important of all is spiritual nourishment. The Bible is
our best source for living a godly life. It offers something for everyone.
Like attending a buffet, we can browse through the chapters and find
appropriate verses for our needs.

For wisdom on good living, consider the book of Proverbs. Feeling
down, praise God with verses from Psalms. Want to be a better disciple
of Christ, delve into the book of Acts. Need to learn more about the life
of Jesus, read pages from the first four books, Matthew, Mark, Luke
and John. But most important of all, you will discover how Jesus' death
on the cross paid the price for our sins. If we put our trust in Jesus, His
resurrection assures us of spending eternity with Him. That's the best
choice and the greatest gift.

A buffet meal of delicious food may satisfy us for a few hours, but
filling ourselves with the Word of God will have lasting effects.

Listening to Jesus: Devotion 1

In this manner, therefore, pray:
Our Father in heaven,
Hallowed be Your name.
Matthew 6:9 NKJV

Jesus speaks to me of FATHER
OUR FATHER

When you call Me Father
it warms My heart as it warms your heart.
For you see,
this is what you were meant to call Me
from the beginning of creation.
Father speaks of many things:
It speaks of a oneness between Me and you
for we are family.
It speaks of the bond of love between us.
It speaks of a teaching
and learning relationship between us.
It speaks of your willingness to learn from Me.
It speaks of My desire
to lead and protect you under any circumstance.
The word Father says that
My love will always be there no matter
who you are or what you do.
Remember the story of the prodigal son;
My love for the son never faded.
When you call me Father,
we both declare that you are My son
I am proud to have you as My son.
Father speaks of a God who loves,
For God so loved the world.
I am not a God to be carved on stone
to be placed on a mantel,
for Father says I am a God of relationships.
I am not a God to go along side of other gods,

for Father says I am the only God,
for there can be only one Father.
There are those who find it hard to call me Father,
because of their earthly fathers,
but remember I have overcome the world.
There are those who find it easy to call me Father,
and so it should be.
In the word Father the human and the divine become one,
but you are never God.
When you call me Father
what you should see in me are-
tenderness, mercy and forgiveness.
When you call me Father
you will feel My tender arms surround you to bless you.
To bless means —
to say good things.
When you know Me as Father
healing begins to happen in your life,
for you no longer need to fight your own battles.
When you come to know Me as Father,
you then come to know yourself.
When you come to know yourself,
you come to Me in repentance,
therefore seeking forgiveness.
It is then as your Father,
I pronounce the absolution on you,
declaring that you are forgiven,
for your sin is paid for by My blood.
When you use the word OUR
it means that you are not alone
on your pilgrimage on earth.
OUR means that you are part of a body
that is united in Me as Father.

Give a Golden Apple

Like apples of gold in settings of silver Is a word spoken in right circumstances. Proverbs 25:11 NASB

My husband is a college professor. He loves his job—some days.
Good days are filled with pleasant news:
- a student receives a prestigious internship
- a clinical instructor compliments the skill of his students
- a former student drops him a note to say he landed the perfect job thanks to his letter of recommendation
- the administration is pleased that program enrollment is up
- all the students pass the certification exam on the first try

Bad days are filled with unpleasant news:
- students gripe about their clinical assignments
- the network is down so his computer is unavailable but his deadlines have not changed
- a student with a grudge rips him to shreds in the end of course evaluations
- a clinical instructor reports that a student is making poor choices
- the class average is extremely low after a relatively easy exam

I remember watching students on old television shows bring apples to their teachers as a sign of appreciation. Maybe it is time to revive that tradition. Instead of real apples, you can bring your professors apples of gold. Speak those words of appreciation. Tell them how much you learned in class. Let your professors know how much you grew as a student by the projects they assigned. Thank them for all those late nights they spent preparing lectures or grading research papers. Your words can turn bad days around.

One important thing about apples—they have seeds. When you give a gold apple of appreciation, the seeds within that apple produce fruit. Those seeds produce the fruit of encouragement, renewal, and satisfaction. That fruit makes your professor better for his family, friends, and the next class he teaches.

So please take a little bit of time before you leave campus to thank your professors, preferably in writing so they can reread it on those bad days. The golden apples don't cost you anything, but to your professors they are priceless.

Different Relationship with Parents

*Every year his parents went to Jerusalem for the Feast of the Passover. When
he was twelve years old, they went up to the Feast, according to the custom.
After the Feast was over, while his parents were returning home, the boy
Jesus stayed behind in Jerusalem, but they were unaware of it.*
Luke 2:41-44 NIV

Every year Jesus' parents went to Jerusalem for the Feast of the
Passover. Mary probably carried Jesus in her arms as an infant, bounced
him on her hip, and watched him toddle along when he learned to
walk. Every year, without fail, this family could be found on their way
to Jerusalem. How was Mary to know that this year, when Jesus was
12 years old, would be so different from all the others? How was she to
know that after this trip she would lose a part of her son to other causes?

When Jesus' parents missed him they first assumed he was with
his friends. But unable to find him they returned to Jerusalem. Listen
to the panic in Mary's voice when he was discovered teaching in the
temple. "Son, why have you treated us like this? Your father and I have
been anxiously searching for you." When he tried to explain they did
not understand what he was saying to them. Things were changing for
Jesus and his family. The relationship was no longer the same. He had
a higher calling from God on his life now.

Perhaps you are in a new season of life as Jesus was. Perhaps it is
causing some misunderstanding between you and your parents. Jesus'
response to this changing situation was an attempt to help his parents
understand. When they didn't, scripture says he was obedient to them.

Even though Jesus was not Mary's little boy anymore, he still obeyed
and showed respect to them. However, he had entered the season of his
ministry and would be following God's voice primarily from now on.

Prayer: Lord Jesus, help me to follow your example as my parents
and I adjust to the new seasons in my life. Amen.

Finals Week

I don't believe in all-nighters. Never have. But I know it's finals week and the all-nighter with a side of energy drinks combo is the craze that your roommates and classmates partake in.

Finals week attacks students with a variety of emotions: anxiety over exams, sorrow (or elation) when saying goodbye to roommates, friends, and significant others, and trepidation over returning home.

To stay focused on the task ahead of you, you must also keep anchored in your relationship with Christ. I found that a stress-filled finals distracted me from my quiet times. When I neglect my quiet times, I feel out of balance.

Paul tells us in 1 Timothy 4:8 that "the training of the body has a limited benefit, but godliness is beneficial in every way, since it holds promise for the present life and also for the life to come." HCSB

As important as education and grades are, you are not to idolize them. An idol is more than a wooden statue or golden calf that we bow down and worship. Idols come in different shapes and sizes in our society. They are a lot more difficult to recognize than the idols depicted in the Old Testament.

An idol, quite simply defined, is anything we place in higher priority than our relationship with God. Many things fit into this category: physical fitness, significant others, and, yes, grades.

As you come into finals week, remember it's time to show your professors how much you have learned. Many of these grades are weighty with importance because they determine whether or not you graduate, your ranking, scholarships, job prospects, and even future education degrees.

But what does it matter if you gain the highest "A" but lose your own soul? Will God be pleased by your studies if they separate you further from Him?

No. God gives us resources such as higher education to use to better understand Him and this world He created.

As you enter into a week full of essays and exams, take a few minutes to set aside your study cards and outlines, and thank God for sustaining you through another semester.

Ask the Lord not only to sear the information into your brain to ace the test, but to also reveal more about Himself through your subject matter.

Returning Home

Finals were over. I should be happy, right? As I cruised the interstate with my clothes and books crammed in the back of my car, I wasn't certain how I felt. I was relieved that my exams were behind me yet anxious about their results. Thankful to be returning home to "my room" but already missing my roommates.

I knew that my freshman year of college had changed me – forced me to rely on myself rather than run to my parents for assistance and to question the beliefs my parents instilled in me and decide whether they were my own. I looked the same on the outside, but felt a new sense of adulthood on the inside.

Little did I know that returning home that first summer would prove to be a challenge. I had lived my last two semesters as my own adult only to return to a household where I would once again be under the rules of my parents.

Simple verses tend to mold my mind more than I realize. That summer, more so than any previous time in my life, I had to evaluate what "honor thy father and mother" meant. Even though you have possibly lived on campus for your freshman year of college, that doesn't make your parents irrelevant to your life. When you live in someone else's house, you need to obey their rules (unless their rules are against God's rules).

I was fortunate that my parents did not enforce very many rules when I returned home that first summer. Out of respect, when I left the house I would tell them where I was going and when I anticipated returning home. If I was going to be late, I would send them a text so that they wouldn't worry.

Since finals are either over or nearing an end, take a deep breath and evaluate what you want to accomplish this summer. Have you been having regular quiet times? If so, good, don't let your summer schedule get you off track. If not, get started now, don't put that off until the fall. Before you know it, the summer is gone and you'll be back in the routine of the school year.

Listening to Jesus: Devotion 2

But the fruit of the Spirit is love, joy, peace, longsuffering, kindness, good-
ness, faithfulness, gentleness, self-control. Galatians 5:22-23 NKJV

Jesus speaks to me of LOVE
THE FRUIT OF LOVE

The love that I give
is the fruit of My Holy Spirit.
It is My Divine love
that is expressed in human behavior.
Greater love has no person that this,
he lay down his life for another.
This is the greatest expression of My Divine Love,
for I gave My life for you.
My Divine Love reaches out to all
regardless of what a person has done.
My Divine Love forgives all
no matter how one has been hurt.
My Divine Love helps all
regardless of who they are.
When you receive my Divine Love
it takes all bitter roots of hatred away
and sets you free.
My Divine love puts a protection around you
so that the enemy cannot turn love into lust.
The love that I give through My Spirit
is an everlasting love.
Once you have received it
I will never take it from you.
You may choose to reject it
but I will always reach out with my Divine love.
My Divine love in My Spirit
gives you the ability to choose.
This is the greatest gift I can give to you.
You can choose to accept Me
or reject Me.

You can choose to do good
or do evil.
You can choose to help someone
or hurt someone.
You can choose to love
or to hate.
Being able to choose love
sets you free to be able to love.
Living My Divine Love
becomes a natural instinct
and becomes a part of you
as it is a part of Me.
So I abide in you and you abide in Me.
My Divine Love in My Spirit
is not so much an action
as it is an intuition.
You receive it and do it without your awareness.
When you receive My Spirit
you receive the fruit of my Divine Love.

I Will Wait

I will wait for You and I will know You
I will mediate on Your Word
I will not give up I will not give in
I will lean on my Beloved as He comes calling
I will come
I will come running up the mountain
And even when I get tired and weary I will not stop running
for I cannot bare living another moment without Your presence
I cannot go anywhere
I cannot do anything
I cannot
I cannot
I will wait on You and I will know You
As the way You know the stars in the sky
And the way You know the beats of my heart
Let me have eyes flint on You
I desire to know Your ways
To know Your thoughts
To feel Your heart
Let me see
Open the eyes to see the beauty that is ever waiting to be revealed
I will come and rest in Your warm embrace
I will not look to any other
I will call to You as I walk blindly into the mist coming up from the
shadows leaning on her Beloved
Your Spirit will guide me in all truth and righteousness
I will wait on You and I will know You
Come and claim my heart for it is Yours
You hold the keys
Unlock the depths of this cold hesitate heart and let Your light
breathe life into me
I am Yours
May I be a vessel pouring forth Your fragrance
Speak to me
Speak to these dry bones to arise and take flight
I will arise when You call me

I will arise my Lord
I will arise and I will come
I will wait for You and I will know You

My beloved is mine, and I am his; he grazes among the lilies. Until the day breathes and the shadows flee, turn, my beloved, be like a gazelle or a young stag on cleft mountains. Song of Solomon 2:16-17 ESV

Author Index

A

B

C

D

E

F

G

H

J

K

L

M

Author Index

Martin Wiles 13, 135
Matt Turner 155
Mindy Humphrey 50, 140

N

Nola Passmore 120, 125
Norma C. Mezoe 7, 90

P

Pamela Heemskerk 3, 16
Pan Sankey 65, 133
Pollyanna Sedziol 100, 156

R

Rachelle Moon 77, 102
Randy Bunyard 23, 119
Renae Adelsberger 166, 167
Rhonda Carroll 89, 97
Ruth L. Snyder 104, 112

S

Sandi Somers 20, 21
Sandy Mayle 58, 136
Sarah Lynn Phillips 81, 141
Sharon Niggemeier 111, 126
Sheri Neuhofer 82, 137
Sherry Taylor Cummins 10, 53
Shirley Stevens 61, 142
Steph Beth Nickel 109, 116
Sterling Dimmick 75, 108
Susan E. Greenwood 32, 98

T

Toby Brooks 34
Travis Hart 62

V

Virginia Blackburn 12, 45

Author Biographies

Adele Jones lives in Queensland, Australia. Her writing is inspired by a passion for family, faith, friends, music and science – and a broad ranging imagination. She has had a variety of poems, short stories, magazine articles, devotions and meditations published. Her first novels are due for release in 2014. For more information visit www.adelejonesauthor.com or email contact@adelejonesauthor.com

Andrea M. Smith is a Project Manager for the International House of Prayer in Kansas City. After many trials throughout her life, she hated God. Then at a crossroad at the age of 18, she had a radical encounter with the Lord, and she has never been the same. Her journey has been a roller coaster, going from a 2 year discipleship program in California, to the International House of Prayer University "Media Institute." To a year with Youth with a Mission and back again to KC. She recently married her best friend, whom she met in the media program. Her passions are discipleship, food, travel, worship, writing, and photography.

Andrea Noles is wife, mother, teacher, and blogger at andrealeigh82.blogspot.com. She enjoys inspiring others to nurture and develop their creative gifts the Lord has provided. She lives in North Carolina with her husband and little boy.

Angela Davis is a devotional writer. She has devotionals published in several editions of Penned from the Heart and Mustard Seed Ministries, an online devotional site. She is in the process of writing her own devotional book to be published later this year. When she's not writing, she enjoys reading, walking, Christian music, and spending time with family and friends. You can visit her at www.angeladavisdevotions.com.

A. A. Adourian loves to learn about God and to write about how the Holy Spirit can change our hearts. She is always asking God for more faith to trust Him, and He continues to give her plenty of practice! Her website, http://www.aaadourian.com, is a continual work in progress.

Barbara Gordon lives with her husband of 38 years in a small town in west-central Missouri. Their family includes three grown sons, three daughters-in-law and three precious grandchildren. Barbara retired from a public school system where she was a district administrator. Her days are now filled with babysitting grandchildren and hobbies, which include reading, geocaching and jogging.

Becky Toews has served in ministry for over thirty years as a pastor's wife and mother of two. She teaches English Composition and Public Speaking at Lancaster Bible College in Lancaster, PA. She also conducts public-speaking workshops to various groups and is the author of Virgin Snow: Leaving Your Mark in the World. Becky writes weekly devotionals which she posts on her website at www.beckytoews.us.

Beth Roose is retired from missionary service with OMF. She is a member of the Hillsborough Baptist Church, Auckland, NZ. She is a member of the Christian Writers Guild New Zealand.

Brenda Jason has a heart and passion to serve women of all ages, sharing God's Word while encouraging them to be women after God's own heart. She began serving in the Women's Ministry at Calvary Chapel Oceanside as a prayer servant for the Military Connection Ministry in January 2002. Over time through God's grace and the Spirit's leading she began serving on staff at CCO and has grown into writing Bible study curriculum and devotions for the women's ministry, and teaching Bible study, workshops and conferences. Her favorite place to be when not serving God's kingdom is talking with God in her gardens. Brenda and her husband James have been married for 26 years and have one daughter. You can reach Brenda by email at: ineveryhand@gmail.com.

Brittany N. Boner is a 2007 graduate of John A. Logan College in Illinois. She has attended classes at three other universities as well. Brittany was raised in a loving, Christian home. Because of past and even present battles, Brittany speaks out boldly, unashamed because she is a new creation in Christ (2 Corinthians 5:17). She has a passion to reach other young people who may struggle with their faith and help them learn what it is to have an actual relationship with Jesus, not just a ticket to Heaven. She is a former, part-time worship leader and hopes to continue her ministry in music in the years to come. Brittany has been happily married to Airman First Class Jordan Boner since 2009. They are currently stationed in California.

Bronwyn Worthington graduated from Whitworth University in 1997 alongside her friend Michelle. Both went on to become teachers and have remained close through the years.* Bronwyn resides in Spokane, Washington with her husband. Presently, she cares for their two children while teaching and writing. Samples of her writing can be found at bronwynworthington.com She can be reached at bronwor@gmail. com. *Michelle is referred to in submission 1, Friends Beyond the Books

Bryan Lawrence grew up in a small town in Southern Illinois and lives there to this day with his wife, Brenda. Small town life suits them just fine, having grown up in one and raising their kids in the same town. Bryan was raised in church as one of those kids whose mother played the piano but managed to cast a disapproving look whenever he was out of line. He has served his Lord in the office of deacon, as a Sunday School teacher, and as a worship leader. In his spare time he enjoys time with his family and reading, especially Christian Fiction authors Dee Henderson and Terri Blackstock and the mysteries they write.

Carole Jenks is a 28 year old woman living in Albany, N.Y. She is a two-time graduate of Institute of Children's Literature and currently writes for Union Gospel Press. For more information about her, visit her at her blog at http://carole-jenks1.blogspot.com.

Catherine Sercombe is a wife, mother of three (they've grown up now), creative writing graduate and published author from Queensland, Australia. She manages an education business where she has the privilege of tutoring and encouraging students of all ages to meet their academic goals. Described in publication as a 'writer whose work reflects an infectious love of language', Catherine says, 'From A to Z, surely the best writing begins and ends in God. In the beginning was the Word, and the Word was with God, and the Word was God (John 1:1-2). That's an epidemic worth spreading.' Her email address is csercombe@stairwayed.com.au.

Charlotte H. Burkholder has devotions published in The Secret Place, Penned From the Heart, The Family Digest, Celebrate Life, and others.

Christi Brooks earned degrees from Southeast Missouri State University and The University of Texas at El Paso. After teaching and counseling for a few years, she chose to be a stay-at-home mom. Now she owns a publishing company and is writing a study with her husband titled un/divided. She would love to hear from you at www.chaplainpublishing.com or christi@chaplainpublishing.com

Cindy Evans is a published poet and writer living in the greater Atlanta area. She enjoys serving at Christian companies, seeing faith-based movies, traveling, spending time with her husband and church activities.

Cindy Krall is the wife of "Doc" and mother of three teens. Three times a week she leaves the grind of the daily climb and blogs about the divine at www.doahead-woman.com

Connie Alexander Huddleston earned degrees from the University of Evansville and Purdue. They prepared her to teach in public and private schools, serve as a missionary in Panama, establish a family counseling center, and serve as a children's minister. She especially enjoys writing about prayer. Her articles and stories have been published in numerous magazines and anthologies. She has two sons, two wonderful daughter-in-laws and six grandchildren. Contact: chuddles@embarqmail.com and read her blog at http://cahuddleston.wordpress.com/.

Connie Hughey is a writer, pastor's wife and mother of two young adults, and she can be found letting her Golden Retriever in and out of the house more times each day than she can count. You can read more from her on her blog, 'In the Waiting Room' at www.conniehughey.com. Her email is lockshock007@gmail.com.

Judith "Cookie" White, is founder of The Sounding Board Teaching Ministries (an online women's ministry), Teacher, Speaker and Women's Life Coach. Author of And I Heard God Whisper, "Walk with Me" and Being Led Beside Still Waters. She can be contacted at: www.thesoundingboardteachingministries.com and tsbtm@comcast.net.

Crystal Hayduk lives in Chelsea, Michigan with her husband, two school-age daughters and one dog. Their oldest daughter lives in a nearby city and is a married college student who juggles classes and volunteer work with parenting a beautiful baby girl. Crystal is a nursing instructor and a freelance writer. She enjoys reading and music in her free time, but bravely tags along on outdoor adventures with her family. You can email her at crystalhayduk.ag@gmail.com.

Darla Carthel is a wife, mother, and grandmother. She has a BS and MA in Mathematics and has taught at the college level. She developed an art business where she paints wall murals and other fine arts. Darla enjoys leading a women's Bible study and is an author and speaker. She and her husband live in Amarillo, TX. You may read more about Darla and see samples of her writing and art at darlacarthel.com.

Darlene Rose Bustamante loves inspirational writing and painting biblical scenes on rocks. Believing that each circumstance in life is an opportunity to write and share God's faithfulness with others. Contact her at: Poemsbydrose@gmail.com

Deanna Baird is a wife, mother and writer. She has been published in The Upper Room, Just Between Us and written several stories for the Chicken Soup for the Soul series. You may contact Deanna at Deanna.baird@gmail.com.

Deb Elkink is the author of award-winning novel, The Third Grace. Deb has an MA in Theology, and has posted a literary study of Bible symbols called MOTIFS on her website. Read more about her there: www.debelkink.com. Or jot her a note just to say hi: deb@rolledscroll.com.

Dorsee Bernat's enjoyment of writing began in junior high and continued through high school. Her greatest enjoyment as a writer is sharing spiritual lessons found in everyday life. Although she makes a living as a nurse, she is constantly reaching toward God's call on her life to write. Besides writing, her interests include gardening, reading, and volunteering at a local nature preserve. For the past seven years, she has shared her life with Phillip Kemp. In the end, her ultimate goal is that her writing might be used by God to touch lives and honor Him. If her writing has encouraged you, or if you have a comment, question, or prayer request, please feel free to contact her. Her email address is dorseeb@yahoo.com. She'd love to hear from you!

Douglas Rose lives in Dallas, Texas with wife Esther. He is a journalist and freelance writer for Dallas Morning News, Guideposts, Standard Publishing, and Upper Room. He is an ordained Assemblies of God minister, in Who's Who in Religion, and a member of Academy of American Poets, Texas State Historical Society.

Edwina Cowgill's first published short story, "Kate's Story: A Story of Redemption and Love," was published in 2009 in Count It All Joy, an anthology of short stories from the members of Christian Writers United, Newnan, Georgia. A second short story, "The Front Porch" was published in 2010 in Skinned Knees and Skate Keys, an anthology of short stories based on the writers' childhood memories. She has been the guest blogger on a number of websites, including the Houston Examiner, F.A.I.T.H.: Following Always Intently Trusting Him; The Sara-Ministry.com, the Midsouth Diocese of the Charismatic Episcopal Church and several church newsletters. Edwina blogs regularly on her own site: www.musingsofedwina.blogspot.com. After performing editing work for over thirty years, including copy editor for Jawbone Publishing, Edwina opened Monarch Writing Services in 2011, offering simple and comprehensive edits, proofreading and ghostwriting. For more information, contact Edwina at edwina@edwinacowgill.com.

Edy Sutherland uses outdoor adventure to help others see Biblical principles through another vantage point. She is the author of The WHEE Factor: The RUSH You Get When You Experience God in Everyday Life. Learn more about her ministry atwww.edysutherland.com.

Elaine Given was born in the then Belgian Congo, the middle daughter of three children. Her parents were New Zealand missionaries there until the brutal death of Elton Knauf her father on 23 November 1960 just after independence was proclaimed for the Democratic Republic of Congo. Elaine and Peter served in the same country after marrying. She had two children. They completed their theological studies in the United States. They are now retired and living in Hamilton, New Zealand.

Eunice Porter is a retired state worker who is active in continued learning at Willamette University and community, church and philanthropic endeavors. A mother of three, grandmother of five, she enjoys sewing, tutoring and playing piano/organ. She can be reached at grandmaoe@basicisp.net.

Frances Gregory Pasch's devotions and poems have been published hundreds of times in devotional booklets, magazines, and Sunday School papers since 1985. She has been leading a women's Christian writers' group since 1991. Her book, Double Vision: Seeing God in Everyday Life Through Devotions and Poetry was recently published by Lighthouse Publishing of the Carolinas. Contact her at www.francesgregorypasch.com.

Georgia Reed grew up in West Texas and after earning a Bachelor of Arts in Secondary Education and English Literature from Wayland Baptist University she headed overseas. She taught English in the Czech Republic, Uganda and Texas for over a decade. She currently serves as a mother to two precious daughters and the wife to an amazing husband. She is a freelance writer and a Jesus lover supreme. You can find more of her writing at www.oatmealsmiles.com and can contact her at reedup@gmail.com.

Glen Carlson attended Lutheran Theological Seminary in Saskatoon, Saskatchewan, and was ordained in the Evangelical Lutheran Church in Canada. He did congregational ministry in Northern Alberta from 1965 to 2002. He was the founder and Executive Director of the Chimo Youth Retreat Center (a ministry for street youth) in Edmonton, Alberta for seven years. In 1977 he had the experience of the "infilling of the Holy Spirit." This led him in a new direction of ministry and his specific calling was to bring renewal to the church. Eventually he became the Executive Director of Lutheran Renewal Canada. In 2002 he left congregational ministry and became a consultant in churches in Western Canada and in Southern California. As a consultant he helps congregations who are in transition as they move forward with new vision. He and his wife Joan live in Stony Plain, Alberta. They have two children and six grandchildren. His passions are listening to Jesus through the written Word and exploring new dimensions of worship.

Heather Alexander is a stay-at-home mom of three who lives in Olympia, Washington with her husband Alex, a cranky cat and 8 twitchy hens. She is adjusting nicely to her recently emptied nest, and looks forward to welcoming a son-in-law into the family later this year. She ran her first 5K at the age of 47 and loves to encourage other "women of a certain age" to start running too! Writing has always been a passion and she looks forward to sharing her work in this new phase of life. You can read her blog at www.heather999.blogspot.com

Heather Rodin is mother to six grown children and serves as Executive Director of 'Hope Grows Haiti'. She lives with her husband Gord and her Great Dane Bogart, in Peterborough Ontario. Family needs, charity demands, writing and speaking keep her schedule busy and her life full.

Helene C. Kuoni enjoys writing Christian devotions and short stories. She and her husband John recently co-authored a book: Her Pen for His Glory: The 1860s Verse of Isabella Stiles Mead. She can be reached at Helene.Kuoni@hotmail.com

Janelle Moore lives in Toowoomba, Australia, where she enjoys being the homemaker for her husband and two children. Before becoming a Mum she worked for 19 years as an Accountant. She also loves to read, scrapbook and mosaic.

Janet R. Sady is an author, poet, storyteller and motivational speaker. She is a certified lay speaker in the United Methodist Church. Published in anthologies including: Reflections of the Soul; Love & Light; Falling in Love with You; I Choose You; The Best of Spiritual Writers' Network; Secret Place; Penned from the Heart; Patchwork Path (2 issues.) Magazines: Country Woman; True Story; Alamance; Our USA and Loyalhanna Review Magazines as well as newspapers and other publications. She received best of show for fiction, and blue ribbon for non-fiction in the Silver Arts Competition in 2013. She has won awards for poetry and short stories. She is the author of five books: God's Lessons from Nature, God's Parables and Lessons Book 2, Sacagewea-The Bird Woman, Mr. Bernie's Most Favorite Place, The Great American Dream, and Winston Wants a Home for Christmas. She can be reached at janfran@windstream.net or jansady422.wordpress.com.

Jewell Utt is the Director of a community food pantry. She has worked in Community Outreach Programs for over 20 years and is the Women's Ministry leader at her church. As a speaker and writer, she shares how God works in ordinary people and everyday moments. She is married with three sons: recent graduates of Va. Tech, Rutgers U and Campbell U.

Joan Nathan was raised in Muncie, Indiana where she attended her first college. She has been to college in Chicago (IL), Houston (TX), Garden City (NY), and Stony Brook (NY) as she earned advanced degrees. Now she has earned a Doctorate of Nursing Practice and she lives on Long Island, New York where she is a Professor of Nursing. She enjoys life as a Nurse Practitioner, a Pastor's wife, a mother of six, and a Grandmother of eight, and caretaker of two goldfish. She leads devotions and Bible studies. Inspiration comes daily through activities such as walking on the beach, traveling, photography, painting oils and watercolors, and reading scripture. She has been a community leader, a PTA council president, and a president of her nursing class. Currently a new interest is in reading about family history. Joan can be reached at Profjnathan@gmail.com.

Joshua Whetstine is a pastor and Church planter in the Twin Cities. Father of three. Husband of 15 years. Lover of God and people.

Judy Webb works full-time at her church as Director of Small Groups. She writes for a daily online devotional called Daily Bible Blast, which can be found at dailyreadingdevotional.blogspot.com. She also writes a blog for widows which can be found at www.judithannwebb.com. Judy can be reached at jwebb@ualc.org.

Julie Bowles works in the social services. She returned to college at the age of 49 years young and earned a Developmental Service Worker diploma. Born in England and raised in the Barrie area, wife and mother of two grown men. She is currently employed with a Christian agency supporting adults with exceptional needs. She came to the Lord 12 years ago and began writing devotionals shortly thereafter. When not working and writing, she loves to ride her bike in the great outdoors. She also loves sheep and photography. She came in second place in the 2014 Blog Awards, under Best religion and philosophy category. Her writings are posted on her web site at devotedtothelamb.com.

Kathleen Bradley lives and works with her Pastor husband in Bonita Springs, FL. Her articles appear in "Christian Activities Online," "Upper Room" and "Christ in You" magazines, Penned from the Heart devotional book and "The Downtown Crowd" newspaper. Her booklet, The Fulfilled Life, is in use in Ladies' Bible studies across the USA.

Keela Cooper can be found at www.keelacooper.com. Keela is an English major at Texas Tech University in Lubbock, Texas. When she is not studying, she enjoys reading classic novels and writing her own. Most of her writing incorporates her own personal testimony of what God has done in her life.

Kelly Martin is a graduate of Lubbock Christian University with a Bachelors of Arts in Psychology and a graduate of University of North Texas with a Masters in Education in counseling. She has professional experiences as a middle school teacher and an elementary school counselor. She currently teaches preschool part time and stays at home with her two sons. Kelly attends Experience Life Church in Lubbock, Texas.

Kenda Turner is wife, mother, and grandmother from Cincinnati, OH, who enjoys writing, photography, and walks in all seasons. She's been published in devotionals, anthologies, and children's magazines. Visit her at kendaturner.blogspot.com. Email: kendaturner@gmail.com.

Kim L. Clarke, her husband, and two adult children live in Calgary, Canada. She has a Bachelor of Religious Education degree from Prairie Bible Institute and has been involved in Christian Education in her home church for 25 years. She is a member of InScribe Christian Writers' Fellowship. Kim began writing in 2010, finding it to be a never-ending adventure, learning about life, herself, and God. She was thrilled to have two essays published in Canada's national newspaper, The Globe and Mail, and a short story published in Inscribe's newsletter, FellowScript. This short story went on to be shortlisted for the 2013 Word Award (Word Guild in Canada). She can be reached at kim59@telus.net

Krystalyn Davis is a new aspiring writer who enjoys creating inspirational literature. Her background is in behavioral sciences. She has a Bachelor of Arts degree in Family Studies from Messiah College and a Masters degree in Social Work from Fordham University. Krystalyn has worked and dedicated her life to helping others whether in word or deed. She considers it a privilege to convey God's message of salvation, grace, love, and forgiveness to anyone she meets. Her prayer is that someone's life will be changed. If you would like to get in contact with Krystalyn, please send her an email at ktdconsulting@hotmail.com.

Kristi Hart currently lives in New Prague, MN, where she and her husband serve as church planters with the North American Mission Board. She has a master's degree in Christian Education from Dallas Theological Seminary. She has been writing ever since she could pick up a pencil and has been published in Canvas Magazine and online at Flourish.me (a ministry of the North American Mission Board). Her Bible study book, Ephesians: One with God and One with Each Other has been used by women's groups and seminary wives in Dallas, TX. Currently she serves as editor for Chaplain Publishing and absolutely loves being a grammar-nerd for Christ. She blogs at thebusypastorswife.wordpress.com.

L. June Stevenson retired from the Presbyterian Church in Canada after 24 years as the editor of their denominational mission magazine. In her position she wrote dozens of devotionals for the PCC and other magazines. She freelances now and is the mother of a son and daughter with five grandchildren.

Lanita Bradley Boyd is a teacher, writer, and speaker who lives in Fort Thomas, Kentucky. She especially enjoys mentoring young women, editing, and reading. Read her thoughts about life in her blog at http://lanitaboyd.com/musings. She can be reached at lanitaboyd@gmail.com.

Leigh Powers has had a life-long love affair with the word of God. A writer, wife, and mother of three, she loves seeing God's people pursing an intimate relationship with Christ through his word. She blogs about faith, life and kingdom living at www.leighpowers.com. You can follow her on Twitter at @leigh_powers or e-mail her at contact@leighpowers.com.

Leslie Winey lives in Indiana, works for a newspaper full time and writes in her spare time. She desires to present truth and glorify God through her writing. She is a wife, mother and proud grandmother of six and counting. Leslie enjoys worshipping and being active at her church, reading, taking walks and babysitting.

Linda Bonney Olin is a farm wife, artist, and late-blooming writer of plays, songs, puppet skits, fiction and nonfiction—whatever the Holy Spirit assigns. Her poems and devotions have appeared in literary and devotional magazines, anthologies, and online publications. Her books include Songs for the Lord: A Book of Twenty-Four Original Hymns and Faith Songs; The Sacrifice Support Group: A Dramatic Comedy for Lent; Giving It Up for Lent: Bible Study, Drama, Discussion; and Transformed: 5 Resurrection Dramas. Visit Faith Songs at www.LindaBonneyOlin.com to learn about Linda and her work, and find a variety of resources for writing, ministry, music, and more. Contact Linda@LindaBonneyOlin.com or Linda Bonney Olin-Author on Facebook.

Linda McCutcheon has a passion for helping women to be all they can be amidst the pain and loss in life. For 12 years, she raised her daughters as a single mom, but recently re-married and enjoys her new start with Bill. She is available for speaking and is currently writing a book for Single Moms. Visit her blog at singlemomsurvivalsuccess.com and her Facebook page at Linda R McCutcheon.

Lisa Evola is a writer and content coordinator at A Beautiful Life Ministries. Her relationship with the Lord has opened many doors that she never would have considered otherwise, and has brought immense peace and purpose to her life. You can find her writing most often at www.abeautifullifeministries.org. If you have a question or a comment please contact her at abeautifullifeministry@yahoo.com.

Liwen Y. Ho lives in California with her husband (who was totally worth the wait) and their son and daughter. She has a Bachelor's in Psychology from UC Berkeley and a Master's in Marriage and Family Therapy from Western Seminary. Learn about her life as a recovering perfectionist at http://www.2square2behip.com or connect with her at mamaho@2square2behip.com. She would love to hear from you!

Lydia E. Harris enjoys spending time with her family, which includes two married children and five grandchildren. She writes the column, "A Cup of Tea with Lydia," hence her grandkids call her "Grandma Tea." Focus on the Family's *Clubhouse* magazines for children publish Lydia's recipes, which she develops and tests with her grandchildren. Lydia has contributed to eighteen books and is the author of *Preparing My heart for Grandparenting*. She holds Bachelor and Masters degrees from the University of Washington and has taught home economics in the public schools.

Lynn Hookway is following her passion of writing to encourage others. She is a budding author with some success in publishing articles and is currently writing her first book. She and her husband live in Calgary, Alberta, Canada. They have four children and soon will have their first grandchild. To connect with Lynn, please visit her website at www.lynnhookway.com.

Margaret Steinacker, Winamac, IN has two books published, as well as writings in several Christian devotionals and editing of a book about her Dad. Margaret graduated from Olivet Nazarene University in 1968. She served beside her husband as keyboardist for 44 years as he led worship. After 30 years as a GED teacher, her first book, Fearless Teaching from a Grocery Cart, details her stories of teaching in a county jail with only a grocery cart as a desk. Her newest book, Unending Praise: 90 Devotions with Ask and Ponder, Prayers, & Journaling in the Psalms, was published in July 2013. Offering 90 days of devotions, you'll find this book gives you the opportunity to improve your worship, your witnessing, and your devotion to God. Margaret can be reached at steinmag@gmail.com. Her books are available on Amazon.

Mark Hughey is a pastor from the Chicago suburbs who loves Jesus, his wife and his family. You can reach him at pastormarkhughey@aol.com.

Mark Spruill lives in Duluth, GA. He has been married to Tammy for over 31 years. They have three adult children and more blessings than they deserve. The purpose of his life is "that I may know Him" from Philippians 3:10. He blogs at http://markspruill.com.

Marsha Hood is a retired English/reading teacher and keeps busy by writing, reading, and enjoying family and friends. She belongs to several writer's groups and the Pennsylvania Poetry Society. She is published in Penned From the Heart, Time of Singing, the Pittsburgh Post-Gazette, and The Upper Case.

Martin Wiles is a "preacher's kid," author, and minister who understands the struggles believers face. He can be followed on Love Lines From God (www.love-linesfromgod.com) Wiles has authored *Morning By Morning, Morning Serenity*, and *Grace Greater Than Sin*. He and his wife Michelle reside in Greenwood, South Carolina. His most recent book is *Grits & Grace & God*.

Matt Turner is a current college student and will be starting at Southeast Missouri State University this Fall 2014. He plans to major in Athletic Training. He spent three years at John A. Logan College taking general studies until he figured out exactly what it was that he wanted to do with his studies.

Mindy Humphrey is a daughter of the King empowered with His grace and mercy. She loves to study God's word. Mindy is passionate about encouraging others to study God's word to discover His truths for themselves. She is the wife to a compassionate and patient man who knows how to bring out the best in her. Mindy is blessed to be a homeschooling mom of four boys. Camping, coaching, swimming, biking and cooking are some of her favorite free time activities. Mindy firmly believes that starting the day with God's word and coffee are the keys to following God's will for the day. You can find more about Mindy and her writings at www.breathingingrace.org.

Nola Passmore has a PhD in psychology, a Graduate Diploma of Arts (Creative Writing) and a Certificate IV in Christian Ministry. She taught psychology at a regional university in Australia for more than 20 years. She and her husband Tim now run their own freelance writing and editing business called The Write Flourish. She has a passion to share what God has done in her own life and to encourage others to do the same. Her poetry, devotions, true stories and short fiction have been published in various magazines, journals and anthologies. Email: nola.passmore@westnet.com.au; Website: www.thewriteflourish.com.au.

Norma C. Mezoe writes from the small town of Sandborn, Indiana. She is active in her church in a variety of roles. Norma became a Christian at the age of fifteen but didn't grow spiritually in a significant way until a crisis, at the age of thirty-three, brought her into a closer relationship with the Lord. Norma may be contacted at: normacm@tds.net.

Pamela Heemskerk found writing took her by surprise while recuperating from an illness. She prefers writing non-fiction and has a passion for art, children, and educating people about hearing loss. She works as a physical therapist with young children with disabilities. Contact her at pgheemskerk1@gmail.com.

Pan Sankey: wife of Bob, mother of three, grandmother of 10. She has enjoyed writing for the last 30 years in various venues: poetry, skits, Bible study guides, devotionals, and such. There is no end of delight in discovering that the Creator of all creation and creativity gives us new ways of knowing Him and provides us ways to reach out and touch others' hearts with the written word as He Himself has done.

Pollyanna Sedziol is widowed with five children, nine grandchildren, and four great-grandchildren. She has been a published poet for 50 years. She is a retired Registered Nurse and volunteers for the Used Book Depository, a ministry of her church that sends Bibles and Christian books overseas. Two of her grandchildren will graduate from college in May this year; five have graduated and are working in their chosen fields.

Rachelle Moon is a wife and mama of four teenagers, is a small town Postmaster and an occasional farm hand. She enjoys cooking and running, with high hopes of completing a marathon this year. She believes in living a life marked by the grace of Jesus. Find her on twitter rachellemoon505 or rachellemoonblog.com, where she occasionally blogs.

Randy Bunyard is currently the Associate Pastor at The Heights Fellowship in Lubbock, Texas. Randy has been working with students for over thirty years as a teacher, coach, counselor, principal, and minister. Randy is an avid baseball fan and has run seven marathons. Randy has been married to Mina for 34 years and enjoys investing in the lives of others as they pursue being disciples of Christ.

Renae Adelsberger lives in Jackson, TN with her husband Kevin whom she met in college. Her career is in insurance but her calling is to disciple young females to follow Christ whole-heartedly. You can read more from Renae or invite her to speak at your college group at www.pedestriangod.com.

Rhonda Carroll is a pastor's wife and mom to two beautiful girls. One of her passions is to help others grow in Christ through the study of God's word and by following God's design for healthy living. She also enjoys writing and teaching healthy living cooking classes. For more information, please check out her blog at www.fromthebibletothetable.com.

Ruth L. Snyder lives in northeastern Alberta, Canada with her husband and five children. She graduated from Prairie Bible College and now serves God as a wife, mother, music teacher, and writer. Contact Ruth at rls67@mcsnet.ca and http://ruthlsnyder.com.

Sandi Somers has been a teacher in rural and city environments and in Colombia, South America. Most recently she taught English as a Second Language, where she met immigrants from a wide variety of cultures. She lives in Calgary, Alberta, Canada.

Sandy Mayle is a freelance writer with a focus on knowing God and drawing closer to Him. Sandy and her husband, Dave, live in northwest Pennsylvania. Email: dasmayle@gmail.com.

Sarah Lynn Phillips and her husband, Barry, have been married 35 years and are blessed with three daughters and a grandson. Sarah is a freelance writer and the editor of *The Women's LINK*, a resource for women in her church and community. Visit her blog, Penned Without Ink, at sarahlynnphillips.com.

Sharon Niggemeier is a wife and mother of two daughters from Long Island, NY. She enjoys reading, spending time upstate in rural NY, and being adventurous. Her many roles include, assistant professor of nursing, bible study co-facilitator, former Sunday school teacher and parish nurse. She has been published in Penned From the Heart vol. 20. and is currently working on another devotional project. To contact her, email to: Sharon1700@verizon.net.

Sheri Neuhofer lives in Chesapeake, Virginia with her husband and son. A freelance writer, Sheri has a deep passion to share the hope and healing she's found in Jesus Christ through short stories, dramatic skits, and devotions. She currently serves as an intercessor on her church's prayer team and as a mentor for young women. Three of her devotions were published in the 2014 edition of Penned from the Heart, a 365 compilation of devotions. In the summer of 2012, she was selected as one of the Top Ten runner-ups in Southern Writers 'Short Story Contest'. You can find Sheri's devotions at, http://atthehem.blogspot.com. Contact Sheri at slneuhofer@gmail.com.

Sherry Taylor Cummins is a writer and speaker in the faith based and business genres. She has authored two devotional books, contributed to several books, newspapers and magazines. She currently is the Human Resources (HR) and Communications Director for a private company in southeast Michigan and is a regular hospitality blogger for Cvent, an event management software company. Sherry has a Bachelor's degree in HR, a Certification in Meeting Management (CMM) and is a Certified Meeting Planner (CMP). You can visit Sherry at www.sherrytaylorcummins.com or write to her at cummins.sherry@gmail.com. She looks forward to hearing about your journey!

Shirley S. Stevens has a Masters degree in English from The University of Pittsburgh. She taught English for 40 years in both the Quaker Valley School District and as an adjunct professor for Pennsylvania State University. She has earned numerous awards for her work in her field, as well as had a plethora of articles and poems published over the years.

Steph Beth Nickel is a freelance writer and editor. She is the co-author of Living Beyond My Circumstances, former Paralympian Deborah L. Willows' memoir. Read more about her eclectic interests at http://stephseclecticinterests.wordpress.com/ or contact her at stephbethnickel@gmail.com.

Sterling Dimmick has a A.A.S. in Journalism and a B.A. in Communication Studies. He has an interest in outdoors activities and photography. He enjoys classical music, literature and studying the Bible.

Susan E. Greenwood is an author, blogger, skit and curriculum writer. Her passion it to help people become rooted and grounded in the Word of God, so, they can live through unwavering faith and find true joy through Jesus Christ. When she is not writing, Susan enjoys life on the farm with her husband Chris and their three sons. You can read more from Susan and connect with her through her website susangreenwood.net.

Travis A. Hart is a church planting missionary with the North American Mission Board (www.namb.net) currently serving in the Minneapolis/St. Paul Metro Area (better known as the Twin Cities) in Minnesota. He holds a Masters of Theology (ThM) from Dallas Theological Seminary, and he blogs and posts sermons at travishart.wordpress.com.

Toby Brooks is an Associate Professor at Texas Tech University. Brooks completed his undergraduate studies in athletic training and completed his Masters and Doctoral degrees at the University of Arizona. He has published eight books, multiple articles and studies, presents regularly at national and international conferences, and also serves as the art director for RPM Magazine. He is active in his church, and in his scant free time, he enjoys drawing, playing the drums, working on cars, and spending time with his wife Christi, daughter Brynnan, and son Taye.

Virginia Blackburn attended Linfield College for three years and graduated from the University of California. She has been married 57 years, is the mother of four adult children, grandmother of ten, and great-grandmother of seven. She is from Boise, Idaho, where she lives with her husband. She is the author of two books: Formula for a Miracle, and a children's book, The Adventures of Roger and Penelope. She has also written for numerous devotional books and children's magazines.

Connect

The devotional authors would love to hear from you. Connect with them by leaving messages on our Facebook page www.facebook.com/chaplainpublishing about the devotions that especially challenged or encouraged you. You can also leave questions there about devotions you disagreed with or would like more detailed information on.

Don't forget to visit the blogs of your favorite devotional authors to see what else they are writing.

And if you have a book or devotional in your heart that is straining to get out, please email me or message me on Facebook. I would love to assist you on your journey to becoming a published author.